HIMALAYAN TOURING WITH MY GURU

Copyright © by T'Om Biehn

All Rights Reserved

No portion of this book may be reproduced in any form without written permission of the publisher or author, except as permitted by U.S. copyright law.

ISBN 97989908142-1-9

This memoir is dedicated to Kathleen, who has been my rock, as I have traveled to Ma India for extended periods six times in the past three and a half years.

And

To the thousands of women and men who have come to the Sattva Yoga Academy in Rishikesh, India, to study under Anand Mehrotra. Here is where a calling becomes a longing, and then a lifetime transformation into contentment and bliss.

And

To each and every person who accompanied me to Gangotri and Ladakh: hikers, bikers, passengers, staff and film crew.

And

As always, Anand-ji Mehrotra, my forever Guru Deva.

Anand-ji in his beloved Himalayas

Himalayan Touring With My Guru

A Pilgrimage to Gangotri: Headwaters of the Great Ganga

And

A Motorcycle Pilgrimage to the Ladakh Region in India

TABLE OF CONTENTS

A PILGRIMAGE TO GANGOTRI: HEADWATERS OF THE GREAT GANGA

1) PREFACE
2) PREPARATION AND ARRIVAL
3) BEING HOME
4) DEPARTURE FROM SATTVA TO GANGOTRI
5) OCTOBER 21ST, 2024
6) THE LONG PATH TO THE HEADWATERS
7) MORNING AT THE SIDE OF MA GANGA
8) TREK BACK TO GANGOTRI
9) MUSINGS ON THE RETURN TO SATTVA
10) BACK TO TUCSON FOR JOY AND BLISS

A MOTORCYCLE PILGRIMAGE TO THE ANDAKH REGION IN INDIA

1) MA INDIA BECKONS FOR THE SEVENTH TIME
2) ACCEPTANCE
3) SHOW LOW MEETS LAKSHMI
4) LORD, LET YOUR PLAN FOR ME UNFOLD
5) DEEPER PREPARATION
6) THE INFINITE, UNIVERSAL PLAN
7) LAKSHMI
8) THAT HANUMAN HEART
9) DEPATURE DAY AT LAST, AUGUST 30TH, 2025

10) ARRIVING AT SATTVA WITH A STRONG BACK
11) TUESDAY, SEPTEMBER 2ND, 2025
12) WEDNESDAY, SEPTEMBER 3RD, 2025
13) IT BEGINS WITH A SURPRISE DEPARTURE
14) LEAVING ANDAZ
15) CHOOSE YOUR MOTORCYCLE AND LET'S GO!
16) OUR FIRST TWO-WHEELED TOUR
17) LAMAYURU, LADAKH, INDIA
18) BACK TO LEH
19) SITTING ON KHARDUNG LA, AT 18,379 FEET
20) NUBRA VALLEY, LADAKH, INDIA
21) THE LONGEST RIDE TO PANGNG LAKE, NEAR THE CHINESE FRONTIER
22) PILGRIMAGE TO T'OM ON THE ROYAL ENFIELD HIMALAYAN
23) EXCITING DAY IN LEH
24) LEH REGION BUDDHIST TEMPLES
25) FLYING BACK TO SATTVA-IN THE FLOW
26) TRYING FOR SATTVA AGAIN
27) INDIRA GANDHI INTERNATIONAL AIRPORT
28) THE LAST LEG, AS INTEGRATION BEGINS
29) HOME IN TUCSON AND AFTER-THOUGHTS

A Pilgrimage to Gangotri: Headwaters of the Great Ganga

PREFACE

Any opportunity I have to travel to India is a joyous gift. To travel to India and return to the site of my spiritual awakening is a life blessing. To travel with Anand-ji, my Guru Deva, to sacred places and the spiritual vortexes that beckon him, sustain the joy and blessings, and the further opening of my heart to the Inner Divine. He is not your average run of the mill Guru. No wild, lengthy hair and beard flowing down his chest. No saffron robes or shaved head. Nope, he is a 43-year-old man, modern in every expression of the word, a true citizen of the world. He is simply one possessing the ancient knowledge of the Himalayas shared with him by his Master for the entirety of his youth. Anand-ji is a Master, a Teacher and Guru known around the world for his insights, knowledge and ability to share the 5000-year-old teachings in a manner that is accessible to every person.

When I am with him, his teachers and other yogis schooled in his tradition, all is right with the world. The awareness and spiritual gifts that he shares have brought me unspeakable happiness.

I first stumbled into his universe via his award-winning documentary, The Highest Pass, a multi-segment observation of him taking his students on a motorcycle tour to some of the world's highest roads and holy temples. I had a chance to get to know him through the film before I had ever met him through in person. I intuitively knew that he would have the answer to the question I have had as a 25-year yoga practitioner...**What is behind the veil of yoga?** I know there is something deeper here, but it seems to always have been just out of my grasp. Yet, with his shared knowledge I received those answers and so much more.

Those who have studied under Anand-ji witness the changes in their lives (and of their students at home) daily. All who pass through the gates (either physically in India or online) of the Sattva Yoga Academy will attest to the profound knowledge and understanding that results. All have access to hundreds and hundreds of online classes and a cornucopia of videos of his teachings. What has not been explored is the deep and meaningful change that takes place in those who absorb all this sacred learning. He lays it out in a manner and process that people from scores of countries can understand, implement and bring into their hearts. This is a story of how one man received, perceived and took to heart and soul these learnings.

And so it was when I received an email announcing his next spiritual journey, I didn't hesitate in signing up. The last pilgrimage I joined him on, again deep into the Himalayas, was to Badrinath and the famous Shiva temple there. It is the purported spiritual home of the greatest Guru of them all, Babaji. The trip brought me closer to my true self and offered answers to many questions I had about this new Yogic life I was living. After all, the Himalayas are not about skiing or winter sports, but spiritual growth and enlightenment!

The world over, people know about the sacred nature of the Ganges, or as they call it in India, the Ganga River or more often Ma Ganga. Literally millions flock to the river, year after year, to bathe and submerge themselves in this holiest of holy manifestations of Ma Nature. Its source, its headwaters, near the isolated village of Gangotri are considered one of the most sacred places on the planet. This is where Anand-ji was taking us.

I am going to take you on the entire journey with me, day by day, hour by hour. I will open my heart to you and offer up my perceptions in an open and truthful manner as I can. To many people India is a scary, third world country, with the largest population of any county on earth. To me it is Home, a place where all are welcome, where spirituality is infused in daily life and celebrated openly. I kiss the ground whenever I get off the plane at Indira Gandhi International Airport in New Delhi. For here there is always adventure, growth, fundamental spiritual awareness and a billion smiles awaiting me. So, thank you for joining me. Let me take you by the hand into the incredible Himalayas of India.

Preparation and Arrival

From my home in Tucson, Arizona, India is on the exact opposite side of the world. The time difference is eleven and a half hours. While the material world in India is vastly different than that in America, it is also the same in many respects. Lots of people, traffic craziness, gargantuan international airports, ever present media, and billions of people striving to get by day after day, either in abject poverty or enjoying the fruits of the world's fastest growing capitalistic economy, or every possible economic layer between the two.

It is a long flight, sixteen and half hours, from JFK Airport in New York City. It takes quite a bit of preparation. When I first went to Sattva in Spring of 2022, COVID was just finishing, and getting a visa was challenging, all online, and seemingly complicated. I knew I would be going back again and again, so I applied for a five-year visa, and I am so glad I did. After overcoming countless technical challenges (the other story of my life it seems), the visa was granted, and I printed everything and put it with my travel docs. Months later I would be deplaning in India for my seven-hour car ride to Rishikesh, the celebrated home of yoga. Three more trips followed in quick order.

Having all that experience under my belt now, this trip would be easier. Basically, I just had to send in my application for the trip to Badoni, the man of many talents and incredible organizational skills at Sattva and book my airplane ticket. As readers of my previous book, *Living Fearless*, know, I have travelled for work and pleasure extensively throughout my life and accumulated millions of frequent flyer miles. Now that I am retired, I get to bring them to bear! At my age, with over 2 million actual flight miles travelled, coach travel no longer suits me so, I searched out a premium economy class ticket to DEL

(New Delhi). While not business class with your own pod and full lie flat capability, premium economy offers an additional 8 inches between you and the person in front of you, a seat that reclines maybe six inches and is two inches wider. That would be fine.

Ten years ago, I discovered the benefits of Ambien when traveling on long flights and overcoming jet lag…I would be AOK! I cashed in 109,000 American Airlines miles for the trip from Tucson to Dallas to New York to Delhi. 24 hours total travel time.

Now I needed to book my trip home and I got lucky! I would continue traveling eastbound, so as to go completely around the world. It would be my eighth around the world trip! I found an amazing fare of 129,000 miles for a business class seat on Singapore Airlines, one of the world's great airlines. I ticketed…Delhi to Singapore to Los Angeles. 23 hours total travel time, taking me through the glamorous Changi airport in Singapore and a short layover at the Narita airport in Tokyo.

Now it was time to prepare the trinity: my mind, body and soul. My last visit to India was in January of 2024 and much time has passed for me. It was time to flex my spiritual muscles. My routine had remained the same. Up meditating for 30+ minutes before sunrise. After being at my side during meditation, Koko, my golden retriever, was ready for the walk. We did two to three kilometers in my neighborhood, which gave me more than enough time to do my japa practice, repeating various mantras 648 times, counting away each one on my mala necklace. Twice a week, Kathleen and I would go down to the river (really a wash that only ran three or four times a year during our monsoons) where there was a lengthy and flat bike / walking paved trail, and we would put in four miles.

I had been doing a daily yoga practice on my new outside platform which overlooked the mountain and desert landscape, right up until the 105 degree heat set in for the summer. That sent me inside, to the ground floor yoga area at my home. I had given myself the sadhana of doing one a day of St. Karen's online practices. St. Karen is a gifted and highly spiritual teacher that taught at my 200 and 300 hour classes and joined the Badrinath pilgrimage, at the Rishikesh campus. She has scores of classes uploaded on SattvaConnect.com.

St. Karen, my primary post-Sattva yoga teacher and great inspiration.

When we graduated from our Master's training in January, we were given online access to the entire Masters program that was taught in person and on the web in Winter of 2021, in the height of COVID. My great friend, inspiration, mentor and dedicated teacher / yogini, Silvi, had encouraged me to begin this class. She had done it and felt it was an outstanding tune up to our January Master's class. I dug in. It is 81 separate videos covering everything we did in January 2024. Of course, there was duplication, but Anand-ji's Journeys and Wisdom Talks are always different and never the same. I dove in. I wanted, above all things, to be prepared for what was to come on this upcoming spiritual trek.

I have been working with the japa mantra Sat Chit Ekam Brahmana for the past month or so. Sat – Truth, Chit – Consciousness, Ekam – the Bija sound for Brahman, Brahmana – the Omniscient, Omnipotent, Compassionate creator of the Universe. After Masters, I have really been tuning in to the Brahman consciousness, leaning hard into it, acknowledging the Grace that flows from it and being cemented in the knowledge that I am engaged in that flow, a willing participant, on bent knees of bhakti love, floating in that divine river. The freedom that comes from accepting that my life is in Unity with the cosmic consciousness which creates boundless bliss, freedom from care and worry about "what will be".

That being said, I am realizing that it has been 6 months since I last left for India, which gives me a little time to devote to analyzing what has happened to me, spiritually in that time. Surely, my Master's training was the peak of my knowledge in this Lila world I am now inhabiting. When one leaves any training at Sattva, there is always a period referred to as integration, where one's mind takes some time to sort out, not only the entire experience, but also the floodwaters of information that everyone is confronted with. And the integration is at odds with what Anand-ji calls habit energy...that is where all that you have learned in India and desired to implement in your life slowly dissipates into the old ways and habits that you have always had of thinking and acting.

For me, after the 200 hour teaching, integration was long and slow, the abundance of new knowledge took maybe three months to filter through and gain residence in my mind. The habit energy was working hard also...old habits are so comfortable and easy to fall into. The lower mind supports this as it ever tries to "protect" us, shielding us from "new and improved" ways that could hold potential unknown harm. Habit energy mirrors the negative bias that the lower mind always carries along with itself and helps support the push back from change. And, of course, the habit energy continues to proclaim that there is just too much energy, work and effort to allow the integration to fully infuse itself into our psyche. Take it easy! Chill! It is so much easier to put your feet up. relax and do nothing.

So how to beat habit energy? Well, by doing exactly what it is pushing back against. Stay strong in your study and practice. Do the work of letting the change happen. Without fail, make meditation a daily practice...twice a day if possible. Get a japa routine going and stick with it. Do asana practice daily. Go through your textbooks and do three or four Kriyas a day until you have done them all and then start over. Engage in SattvaConnect with the hundreds of classes offered, giving you support and engagement. You simply have to do it, especially at the beginning, trying to keep that blissful feeling with which you left the campus. That wasn't a dream, but a step ladder to inner peace and the cosmic doorway.

Post 200 hour yoga teacher training, I stayed at it. I read and read. All of Anand-ji's books were devoured and I was referred books from other students *(some of the best referrals were from Virginie, a French Sattva mentor of mine)* and I found others on my own. I kept my mind engaged in the spiritual realm. I listened to Dharmic musicians like Shantala, Krishna Das and Deva Premal. And I worked hard to fill my heart with love. To know that every single human being out there has the divine within, no matter how tamas their gunas seemed or what my judging lower mind was telling me. Just keep loving!

It paid off. As I arrived at Sattva again four months later and engaged with my 300-hour teachings, I was coming from a much higher place. I understood so many of the terms, the rituals, the mantras, even had a better handle in picking out some of the Sanskrit words and phrases. Instead of questioning and wishing for further explanation of Anand-ji's Wisdom talks, I was nodding my head and getting it, feeling like I had experienced some of what he was talking about. I was struggling with some things like koshas and chakras (at least until I had my Kundalini Awakening!) but, I had sincere and positive thoughts that all of these deep things would come into the light as I studied and prepared myself to receive them.

The post 300-hour period was beautiful. My integration went much more rapidly, due to the solid foundation I had been working from, and pushing back on the habit energy was noticeably easier. That period was not without challenge though, as life seemed to want to put me to the test, to hold my new beliefs up to the light and see if they could stand up to the fire. I was challenged with finding a local studio where I could teach. I had personal challenges. Leaning into the Dharma always provided a pathway to victory or, if not a perceptible victory, then a clear sense of understanding that I cannot simply frame my life to go in the direction that I want it to. I learned I just must let go. To roll with it. To understand that obstacles are just tests in our path to glory. They are put there for a reason and once one can come to terms with that, one can move forward to remove them with the knowledge that when they are overcome, I will be better for it and will have evolved and transcended as a result. Anand-ji says, "Ask not why this has happened **TO** me, but why it has happened **FOR** me."

That sadhana made it easy when my beloved yogis from Sattva started urging me to join them in the Masters. I had signed up for the Badrinath pilgrimage before I left the 300, so I was quite focused on prep for that, thinking the Masters was only 2 months later and I could easily hold off a year on that. The problem was IT WAS ALL TOO GOOD! My integration was going beautifully, and my life was changing in such a full and sublime manner. I had it all going off and I was garnering so much, digging in and receiving, just what I had spent 20+ years searching out to find…why stop? Why put off anything? I was retired, I had the time, and the inertia / energy was surely there. It only took a few more messages of urgings from my beloveds and I signed up for January 2024 Masters.

To be sure though, there were some underlying currents from within moving me along. It was the desire to spend as much time as possible in the presence of my Guru Deva. There was no doubt in my mind that he is an enlightened person, that he has been righteously taught and has accepted the Path. His teacher, Maha-ji, was a brilliant and great Master, and his Master before him. I had never seen any indication of any negative aspects of Anand, and at this point, had spent quite a bit of time with him. Frankly, I had deep concerns about him withdrawing, handing over the reins and going into his own cave. Or, that based on his growing popularity and fame as one of the pre-eminent gurus in the world, he would become inaccessible as a result of the masses coming to learn from him. Sitting in a class with 16 people vs 160 people is quite a difference. Already I had noticed a slight pullback from the number of journeys which he led in my 300 hour vs the 200 hour.

I have spent much time talking with fellow students about this and praying and meditating on it. In the end, I think it is a mountain of my own making. Why am I entertaining these thoughts? It will be what it will be. I am blessed to be one of 400 or so people that have followed through to complete the Masters training. He is my Guru. He will not forsake me. On the other hand, there is a time when all apprentices must pull away from the sheltering wing of their teacher (little did I know then that my time would be coming). Anand-ji lives for teaching, for passing the sacred knowledge to as many people as he can, mouth to mouth, eye to eye, person to person, as has been done in the Himalayas for millennia. However he lives cannot be affected by me in any way at all. I will certainly honor his every decision and continue to be his chela for decades to come. I know he will always be available to me and all of us, and even if he dropped his body tomorrow, he has given us his all. And what he has given us will be here forever.

I have documented my experiences at Badrinath and my Master's training program quite thoroughly in my previous book, *Living Fearless*, so rather than dwell on that further, let me talk a bit more about why I am writing this book. When you have a teacher who changes your life with great and ancient knowledge, it means the world to you. Sometimes it is hard to explain to people how this transformation has taken place and what now? How did this happen and are you sure this guy is not a charlatan, a hypnotist, a magician? Yep, pretty sure. I just feel so deep inside of me that I want to continue to tell the story of what has happened to me. I truly believe that in order to tell that story that I need to share Anand-ji with you, dear reader. Many of you are already his students and don't really need a diatribe on this. I just feel the story needs to be told.

How does all this come about? And who is This Guy? Actually…" Who Is This Guy?" could be a good sub-title for this book. Maybe more to the point would be How has This Guy given you all of this and what are you doing with it?

Anand-ji, my Guru Deva, Master and Teacher

This is what I want to share with you. I want you to live in my shoes for the two weeks of the Gangotri pilgrimage. I want you to feel what I am feeling. Experience the dynamism of the entire traveling group. Gather in Anand-ji's teachings, his buoyant enthusiasm to be traveling to the sacred realms. To watch and see what happens to me as a simple pilgrim traveling with his guru.

And so, I study, I practice, I meditate, I japa, I teach, and I try to open my heart in that Hanuman fashion to each and every person I come across and every situation that the Divine will put in front of me in the next three months. I will be getting on that jet plane in no time. I will be ready. I will be open and receptive. I will be prepared to stand at the precipice of the Himalayas, open my wings and dive into the unknown. I am certain that is where my continued growth will come from. Living fearless, facing the unknown undaunted and accepting it all as an adventure within.

We have just returned from a 5 week vacation in the car (so we can take Koko!) to escape the summer heat in Tucson. Up the spine of the Rocky Mountains and over to Seattle, then back down the Pacific coast. I stayed true to my spiritual fitness, keeping up the meditation and japa, adding in the LMS Master training work as time allowed. Alternating that with asana practice, often in the back yard alley at my daughters, or a spare bedroom at other accommodations. We travelled over 4000 miles with no incident whatsoever. Maybe having a 4 inch brass statue of Hanuman on the dashboard helped with that!

Because of the travel, I missed Anand-ji's visit to the US, his first in ten years. I knew I would be seeing him soon enough. My student, Catherine, was excited to see him live and in person and she attended the LA event. Of course, she was welcomed into the Sattva family by Pamela (my heart felt yogini from the

300 hour) whom I had alerted, and she met many of my beloveds.

And now I am six weeks out! So, the preparation and the dive goes deeper. Mind, Body and Soul. I am finishing the last 10% of the LMS and kicking up my practice. I now have given up on going to yoga studios as I have everything one could possibly need and hope for in terms of classes on SattvaConnect.com. I am comfortable with all the basic array of asana and am finding that I am moving past the desire (or capability) to do some of the exotic ones that are brought forth in studios. I can self-correct or move into a variation on my own as needed. I am practicing with my esteemed teachers from Sattva, including St. Karen, Tomas, and of course, Anand-ji. There are classes posted by many of my fellow teachers with whom I travelled the teaching path.

It was now time to accumulate trekking goods and begin setting everything out for packing for the journey. I needed to buy a large backpack and since this was a one-off deep Himalayan trip, I really didn't feel I needed to get a $500 REI pro one. I searched Amazon and found a perfectly adequate one for $60. As it turned out, we had donkeys trekking all the larger packs up to the campsite, so I could have easily gone for a large duffle that could have been used down the line in my varied travels. That is exactly what my dear Kuwaiti friend, Mishal, did, as he brought in his usual abundant supply of goods, including a 10" thick blow up (via USB hook-up of all things!) mattress. We were all appropriately jealous!

I followed Badoni's provided supply list pretty close and had to also buy a head lamp, a thin thermal mat, some carabiners and a Sony digital voice recorder, which I ended up using primarily to record Wisdom talks by Anand-ji. Having lived in southern Oregon after my 16 years in Hawaii, I was in good shape and stocked up on cold weather gear. During that time, I had purchased an over-the-top, heavy, North Face parka, which served me well on the journey. Catherine had sent me a lovely REI sleeping bag, which, while light (for camping, down to 32F), saved me the purchase of a bag.

I had everything spread out over one of the spare beds in our house and organized as much as possible. Of course, there needed to be room for all of the snacks Kathy had purchased at Costco and Trader Joes, including power bars, dried mango, fruit bars, trail mix, etc. Somehow it all fit.

In my suitcase I needed to bring my non-cold weather clothes for my time at Sattva and Delhi. A couple of weeks prior to departure I had a surprise WhatsApp message request from St. Karen @ Sattva. She was very humbly asking me if I could bring her some good cheese and fine chocolate, as her beautiful Belgian self was pining for those normal Flemish treats, a bit hard to come by in India. Oh my, I loved it! Finally, a chance to repay her for all of the bliss and wonder she had brought me over the years by her presence and in her eloquent and enlightened teachings. I really loaded up a serious stash for her!

In my Addidas daypack I put in my laptop, all the various power cords we can't live without in the modern world, three books, reference materials and all my "can't lose" things like passport, wallet, cash, etc. I was ready.

I managed to stay focused and on point...and today it is October 15, the departure date. Lionel Richie's "Penny Lover" was playing on the radio as Kathleen pulled up to the curb, dutifully dropping me off at the Tucson airport, with Koko, my golden retriever, in the car eyeing the luggage suspiciously, knowing full well I was leaving her behind on another adventure. She would keep Kathleen company during my 18 day absence and they would support each other. Big hugs and kisses and I was over to the American Air counter with the usual questions about, "You are going to India?" from the agent. A flight through Dallas, and then to JFK in New York went quite smooth I deplaned to find the fancy American Airlines lounge at JFK where I could relax in comfort, get in my last US style food fix and chill until departure for Delhi.

You can't pick your neighbors and the same is true on an airplane. The gods were good, in auspicious grace, and I had a lovely Indian gentleman, a devoted Hindu, aside of me on our premium economy section of the plane. He, of course, knew of Gangotri and Gaumukh and was thrilled to hear of my journey. He filled me in on all his religious lineages and we chatted away non-stop. I always like to watch a little Bollywood to get me ready for arrival in India as American always has a good selection of those. Along with some pretty good sleep (Ambien!) the 16 hour flight passed quickly and I found myself deplaning in Delhi.

Home. Home! I am rarely filled with more zeal than when, after months of anticipation, I have landed again in Ma India. I kiss the ground. I am ready! I had taken a few extra custom forms from my last trip, which I had pre-filled out, and hurried the long halls to the top of the big escalator which drops you down in the immigration area. Everyone who has been there, especially yogis, love being greeted by the dozen or so gargantuan hands above the hall forming many of the mudras that we know and love from our Kriya. I looked below and there was not one person in the premium class immigration line. I pulled up and sailed through in no time.

I go straight to the money changers, as we cannot, for some reason, buy rupees in the USA. I never go to the Big Bank areas but have a favorite spot where a regular guy has set up with a simple table, counting machine and copier. I know the exchange rates (XE.com) and they are always the best. We trade religious blessings, and I go to retrieve my luggage. What! My bags are there waiting for me, having already been lifted off the carousel. I put them on my cart and headed for the international arrivals door to look for my driver holding up a sign with my name. I love that the Sattva drivers are always right there and into the parking lot we went, soon to dive into the morning traffic in Delhi.

I am always fascinated with these drivers, country boys from Rishikesh, burrowing into the thick of Delhi, one of the world's largest and most chaotic cities. They never use GPS or maps of any kind. As most Sattvans know, the travel up to Rishikesh can take anywhere from four to seven hours. I always ask the driver when we will arrive at Sattva, and they are ALWAYS right, within 15 minutes or so. The unpredictability of it all makes it an amazing feat in my eyes.

Apparently, Delhi morning traffic is different than most western cities as the government and many commercial operations don't start work until 10AM. So, I squirted out about 9:30 and we were off. Going to Rishikesh, you have never driven through more roundabouts in your life. There must be at least 30-40 in the government center area alone...I get so turned around and lost. Again, I don't know how they do it! The drive to Rishikesh always includes a stop at the driver's favorite dhaba, roadside restaurant.

Nonetheless, after the blur of the city and the immense apartment buildings filling the horizon, there are finally the flowing sugarcane fields, and the city is in the rear-view mirror. You pass through small towns, some Sikh and Moslem areas, and begin the approach to Haridwar. Home to the famous Kumbh Mela where millions assemble every twelve years for a festival on (and in!) the Ganga. Haridwar's giant OM bridge and Shiva statue are landmarks that remind me I are heading into the Himalayas, home of Yoga and the sacred Hindu lands. We flew through Haridwar and then came to the normally slow railroad crossing which is the seeming gateway to Rishikesh. Things started to crawl. We passed the Neem Karoli Baba ashram with the big Hanuman statue in the courtyard and plunged into Rishikesh proper, traffic grinding slower and slower. City life again came face to face with our car and after 45 minutes or so we squirted out of town and crossed the Ganga bridge that takes us onto the bumpy lanes to the very rural Sattva campus. Past the Garuda temple and through the mysterious toll takers, where some drivers fly past, some pay an unmarked toll and others argue and then pay, laughing as they drive on. In 20 minutes, we pull down the driveway into Sattva and I AM HOME at 16:00 India Standard Time, October 17th, 2024!

BEING HOME

17 October 2024

What a joy that the first person I saw was Jemina, my meditation teacher, partner practice regular and one who makes the entire Sattva Yoga Academy work in a seamless manner. Big hugs exchanged and I told her I would be writing a book on the entire experience and asked permission to record Anand-ji's Wisdom talks for reference and deeper analysis. There were fellow master yogis, Paul and Aditi, a couple from Seattle of whom I have become quite fond. Aditi teaches prenatal yoga teacher classes and often has kirtan for us.

The guys grabbed my bags and I shuffled off to my normal room in the cottages, adjacent to Anand-ji's office. Wow! They have been working since my last visit in February! Totally redone bathroom with sparkling new tile walls and floors, freshly painted throughout and all new furniture. Love it!

I next ran into Pennie, a sublime master yogi, who was on the Badrinath trip with us. What joy to have returning pilgrims! I was walking to my dearest friend and advisor on campus, the huge Big Buddha, resting along the river. His area, also, was upgraded with new stone hardscaping laid before him. I was down on my knees before Him immediately, tears streaming in gratitude for His humble and sublime spirit that enabled me to return to my Home. All the safe travels, halfway around the world... I gave up to Him all my trepidations for the trip and they melted away into the surety of a perfect experience. I stayed there fifteen minutes in prayer and reverence.

It was getting close to dark now and I wandered over to the other side of campus where I was shocked to see that the Sattva temple / shrine area had been completely and fully updated! Oh my gosh, it was gorgeous. It now had a beautiful roof over it with sweeping arches and lights. The floor was all marbled in and it looked beautiful. I always thought there should be a more permanent roof over it, but Anand-ji went all in. All future visitors really will have something wonderful to enjoy and a place of beauty in which to have puja, aarti and other gatherings. On the trek, I asked Anand-ji about it. He told me that prior to leaving for his travels to the United States in August, he came up with the design and told his masons they needed to finish it before the pilgrimage. Job beautifully conceived and brought to fruition on time!

Off to dinner and the group started filing in. There was Tomas and Regina,. He was my Lithuanian 200 hour asana teacher, ecstatic dancer and yogi of great inspiration to me. And his Russian wife, who is probably the most experienced Sattva yoga teacher of anyone. She has a spirit that shines as brightly as the Surya. I can listen to her talk for hours. She often brings me to tears with her wealth of knowledge, understanding and most fun laugh. Both have been alongside me for all of my experiences at Sattva.

At this point I was fasting. Between the American lounge at JFK and all of the food they stuff down you on the 16 hour flight, I needed a break. So, I skipped dinner and headed to my room to do some meditating and a gentle Kriya workout. Somehow, I made it to 21:00 before hitting the pillow. My sleep aid (really jet lag aid) helped me to sleep deep and solid, like one always does upon returning Home, until 6AM the next day. I was up and ready for puja. I don't miss those or take it for granted anymore!

The next day, the 18th, was the scheduled arrival day for most of the pilgrims. Puja in the new shrine was elevating! What an addition to the campus! I then wandered over to Shri Buddha and did my meditation in his presence on the lovey, new hard-surfaced area. It was then off to our first yoga journey of the trip, this one being led by Tracy, a woman from the Atlanta area who was currently leading an Ayurvedic teaching retreat on the campus. She really helped get the kinks out and get us all in the flow.

My fast was now over after 24 hours and I enjoyed my typical Sattva breakfast of papaya, watermelon and oatmeal. I walked down to the tiny village by campus to buy some liter bottles of water. They were 20 rupees a piece for a liter . That is 24 cents US each, a low price never to be ever seen in the US. What does something cost? It is a very different metric in India. For example, those of us who need a salt fix can buy any of the ubiquitous bags of peanuts, chips or popcorn that hang in sleeves of 10 in front of every store in India. Those small "convenience store size" bags just hit the spot. They are 10 rupees each. That would be 12 cents US. Really! Is anything in the west 12 cents anymore? Anything? In the states they are invariably $1.79 or so these days. Oy vey.

Nap time approached at that point and my notes said it was an "Anvil Nap", so I guess it was pretty hard and fast. It is how you beat the 12 hour time difference jet lag. I moseyed up to the Rasa café, where they always do the check ins for any events on campus, from teacher training to pilgrimages. Our swag was a nice Sattva T shirt, a canvas carry bag and a truly lovely, large, cotton blanket...pick your design and color. Uma, Alice and Charlotte were on hand to assist, run the show and get everyone signed up.

I was shocked when I headed down to lunch to see Elena, my dear friend from our 200 hour training. She had deeper knowledge and experience than most of us, so at the time, I gravitated towards her aura. We became good friends. She is a Russian Jew by birth, who's family emigrated to Winnipeg, Manitoba, Canada when she was young. Elena is just one of those yogis who "has it". Such a nice reunion and how it foretold a more expansive journey ahead.

I wanted to go to back up to Rasa, where there is always good strong internet, so after lunch, up I went. I happy I was to see Lydia, a deeply spiritual German woman who lives in Queensland, Australia. She has such a wealth of understanding I always enjoy speaking with her. We were together in my 300 hour and Master's training. I took the chance to get caught up with my internet, quite important as I had two of my rental properties up for sale.

This evening was the Welcome Circle, where we sat with the staff, the teachers and all the pilgrims in a circle as Anand-ji spoke and led the comments from everyone as we went around the room. There was a beautiful floral art decoration in the middle of us. Naturally, my tear ducts opened up fully. Everyone spoke to the reason for being on the pilgrimage, their expectations and all honored Anand-ji. My words were along the line of, "The Ganga is a spiritual artery to the heart of Mother India. I am going to the headwaters to open my heart and let that spirit flow through me."

The group flowed over to the havana where we participated in a yagya, which included 108 "Tare Tu Tare" mantras. I threw my selfish self and its monkey mind into the fire and tried to free myself from my attachments to make as much space as possible for the journey ahead. I bowed in deep gratitude for the ever-present Grace in my life, for being Home in Ma India and at the feet of my beloved Guru Deva.

We all flow into the café for dinner. I was thrilled to sit next to Tomas and Regina, to feel the spiritual glow they both radiate and send to any environment they are in. Tomas has meant so much to me on this yogic path. His wife, Regina, has a dynamic pulsating aura, is so deeply spiritual and has such a deep grasp of Anand-ji's teachings. She has been living the Sattvic life for over 15 years. We talked and talked. They had ordered some specialty shoes from the US that would be delivered to my house, and I would bring as luggage to Sattva. Sadly, the boxes did not arrive in time for my departure. I will bring them on my next trip! (Or so I thought.)

The next morning starts with puja in the new shrine area. Jemina took the lead, and it was a sublime start to our first full day as a group. I sat on my lanai of the cottage and meditated, with the serene background of the river and the tropical birds. Home. We gathered into Shakti Hall for our first Journey with Anand-ji. As has been my experience with his journeys in the past year, he laid out many beautiful and simple Kriya exercises to take us away and plant our feet in Ma India. "Go deep, fill your lungs with their full six liter capacity of air." There were simple asana and some partner work and eye gazing, as is normal on the first day for any group at Sattva. I found myself in front of a young German woman, gazing into her blue eyes, feeling so much gratitude for her presence, for the younger generations that are flowing into Sattva, preparing to change lives. We hugged and it was off to breakfast.

Anand-ji spoke about the amazing trip, our incredible journey from the one small cell at conception, through the growth and transcendence of your life, to you finding yourself in Rishikesh, India. It is not easy to get here, it takes hard work, but here you are. That is the Cosmic Consciousness at work...it doesn't just happen. We all glow and float on breakfast.

After puja and meditation was breakfast. I sat with Aditi and Pennie, an RN, and former Delta flight attendant. Now a world traveler, retreat leader and Yogi extraordinaire (such a role she would play in my journey!).

Today was Kathy and my 7th anniversary of our first date! Our calendars never seem to align perfectly for our special holidays and India has claimed me for many of them. Being a good Sicilian from Philadelphia, she celebrated on her end with a Philly steak and cheese sandwich!

And back to the cottage to begin the final packing for the trip. We could leave all our warm weather clothes in our rooms as they were ours exclusively and would not be disturbed while we were gone. The call time tomorrow was 6AM, so everything needed to be thought out, organized and packed up completely tonight, with backpack and day pack to be on the stoop by 5. I was ready.

We got to enjoy a satsang with Anand-ji before lunch and this is what he talked about.

As always, the three mantras to start, after the OMs. He asked for questions and when he finished up with those, ventured into a discussion of pati yatra, the term for pilgrimage. He says a translation is "crossing over to a different state". Pati can be translated as "(1) moving with your teacher, (2) a fixed location such as mountains, rivers and vortexes or (3) state of the conscious Mind. So, it is where prani, your being, interacts with the field. But just being there does not make a crossover. You need to take on all three!"

He reminds us that "India's qualities are on a subtle level, that the quality of the environment generates a particular energetic field. The pilgrimage is also found in the Inner Self. You have to feel, to experience, on the subtler level. We are alone with our own personal experience. No one is responsible for your own experience in yoga, Unity. We are reaching for the Maha Yatra, the Great Experience. Not just climbing and trekking, but a personal, meaningful experience. Ultimately the pilgrimage is part of your life. Everything that happens on pilgrimage is sacred and There is Only SACRED. The Self is the creator of all life."

He touched on home being the place where you feel safe and accepted. No wonder I call Ma India home. Nowhere do I feel safer and more accepted! "Nonetheless, it is impossible to have a life without struggle. From challenge comes growth and evolving. Take the opportunity to crossover. When your life becomes a pilgrimage, it starts to glow with a fragrance."

We cannot give what we do not have ourselves.

If you are sincere, it always comes through.

The Shivalik Mountains, where we are heading, are named after the dreadlocks of Shiva. The holy rivers flow through the crown of Shiva. Wherever we go, the Ganga flows, and we bring life.

Making contact with the Source is simply wherever we make contact. Whenever we are in alignment with the Source that Source flows through us. The flow state is life happening through me, not to me. This flow state leads to the Shiva state, life happening through us as the God consciousness.

After our wisdom talk, I took the opportunity to have lunch with Elena at Avenue 18 restaurant. For each of us, this is the main meal of the day as we both tend to skip dinner. We talked for 2.5 hours, non-stop, like the old friends we are. While we were gone, they changed the daily plan to have the Big trip logistics discussion during our lunch, rather than the scheduled 4PM. We missed the entire overview of the journey, our car partners, hotel info, etc!. When we returned, people asked about our whereabouts saying they were wondering why we weren't there. Change is a constant for all schedules at the Sattva campus, so we just rolled with it. Anyways, it was time for a jet lag nap!

I woke up and wondered over to see what was going on for dinner. It was Tomas' birthday! Birthdays are always a big deal on campus, as the cooks put on their baker's hats and make some birthday cake. It's a big deal as there is rarely desert in the café, save the sugar soaked doughballs, and everyone is excited for CAKE! However, Tomas was staying away from any form of sugar for a spell, so no cake! While he was celebrating (without cake!) I had another chance to have an extended talk with his wife, Regina.

She was glowing, beaming and radiating spirituality as always. I asked her about her length of time that she has been with Anand-ji and she told me 15 years. This is virtually longer than anyone else and there are few who revere and understand him like she does. As always, she shared some insights with me. "Every sentence he says needs to be considered in depth. He is Holy. Nothing comes out that is not deep and with many levels." I took that to heart.

She says lately she has been grappling with the "why" of everything...every action, every thought, every circumstance. Since reading "The Essential Sri Anandamayia Ma" I have come to understand the "why" all relates to God, Brahman, and He is the Why of all things. I am 100% sure Regina knows this but was going on a much deeper level.

Regina then turns to me and says, "T'Om, why are you so hard on yourself? You are a beautiful human being, as is all around you. Relax, live, go with The Flow. You, in particular, know you can't change anything. Consider trying to not work yourself and your world so hard!" And she is right. You know from my book,

"Living Fearless" that I have overcome fear, but that doesn't mean I am not hard on myself.

I love this woman, whose words flow from her in a soft Russian accented sound. She has been in my Guru Deva's life for so long, has absorbed so much, done the work and received the Grace with an open heart. She has a lofty God Consciousness lifestyle to which I would love to aspire. Let it flow...you are on the river, it knows where it wants to take you. And with Regina's glow spreading all over me, I am off to my cottage for a 20 minute WhatsApp chat with Kathy and a hot shower. Yes, hot. My hot water hadn't worked since arrival...the monkeys had been on the roof and were pulling wires and making mischief.

After the entire buildup of coming to India, arriving and diving right into the spiritual realm, I had come to expect that things would start bubbling up and changes, growth and transcendence would become palpable. Sure enough, I went back to my cottage and sat on my lanai and the thoughts started flowing. Having been married twice in my life, once at seventeen for seven years and again at twenty-five for forty-three years, I felt pretty sure I knew my way around the marital universe. With two failed marriages behind me, I felt jaded even considering the option of ever doing it again.

That, however, contrasted greatly with my girlfriend Kathleen's take on the subject. She greatly desires the commitment and security of a marriage...values it above almost all else. I have been quite stubborn about not wanting to fail for a third time. I have pointed out to her that in our neighborhood of older couples, over 80% had listed themselves as single, living together! Our living status together was not at all unusual. I have always felt that once the signature goes on the marriage document things begin a long, slow southerly track.

Kathleen and I have been together for over seven years and we have seen the ins and outs of each other in manifest manners. When one passes seventy plus years of age, the meaning of a life partner starts to take on new dimensions. One begins to think along the lines of "holy shit!" I am no longer a kid or even a middle-ager, and I am going to need someone to take care of me in my dotage and she feels the same way. We don't need someone who is ready to go to the disco and party until the early hours, someone to be a good mother or even someone to be a breadwinner. Anymore, in the Western world, you cannot depend on your children to be your caregivers.

After seven years we can say that we surely know every aspect of each other, rather intimately so. From medical scenarios, dietary lifestyles, outlooks, preferred way of daily living and really, all of the things that make a wonderful and comfortable life together. Why wreck it with getting married? Yet, here, sitting on my lanai at Sattva, in meditative contemplation, it bubbled up! T'Om...quit being so selfish! You have found the one who brings you comfort and to whom you love to bring joy and compassion. This is it! You are not going to retreat to match.com or ourtime.com to find another lover. This is it! You found and have the one...just do it! You have the means to offer her the one thing in life she so desires.

And once that thought emerged, the floodgates of right thinking poured into my Atman. Right then and there I made the decision to ask Kathleen to marry me the day after I returned home. It felt so right. I feel so good.

DEPARTURE FROM SATTVA TO GANGOTRI

20 October, 2024

Up early and we climbed into our cars at 6AM. There were 13 vehicles, all SUVs so we were comfortable for the journey and our luggage fit in easily. As always, Anand-ji's Mercedes SUV was the point of Arjana's arrow, and we flew deep into the Himalayas. What a joy it was to meet my car mates, all the elder statesmen of the group! Bill was from Durango, Colorado and I was acquainted with him from our 300 hour and had also seen him a couple times at various Telluride yoga festivals. Sattva alumni tend to hang together! Then we had Warwick, an Aussie surfer masquerading as a financial advisor (successful on both fronts). I begged off my normal front seat, as my hearing is slowly going and I wouldn't be able to hear the back seat conversations very well from the front.

We knew it was going to be a seven-hour drive, creeping, twisting and turning through the mountains, so we settled in. Guy talk! We talked about travel, wives (girlfriend in my case), and spiritual discussions. Warwick spoke much about his surfing travels and, with my having lived in Huntington Beach, California for 25 years and Hawaii for 16 years, I could easily see he knew many of "the surf spots and people" I was familiar with. I love seeing Aussies on the road as they are, in my mind, the most fun and prolific travelers on earth. I was surprised to hear him say Yosemite (in California) was one of his favorite places on earth!

Bill had lots to talk about, and we discovered our partners have a similar place in our lives. I call it the North Pole / South Pole relationship. Both of us have mates that are not interested in Yoga, Sattva and the alternative life whatsoever. (This would change on the upcoming motorcycle tour where Beth joined Bill and the rest of us). Both of us are deeply mired in that world. Somehow, we meet at the equator, creating beautiful and sustainable relationships.

It is about 280 kilometers (175 miles) to Gangotri from Sattva. If you Google map it, you will see an estimated driving time of seven and a half hours. That is an average of (23 miles) 37 km per hour. I suppose that gives you an idea of how twisty and turny the roads are when you dive into the Himalayas. For the most part the road winds along the Ganga and her tributaries as she cuts her path to the sea. Up and up, switchback after switchback. Past towns, villages and hamlets, large and small. The sky gets bluer and the scenery more vivid as the snowcapped, majestic mountains start coming into view. The group began getting a little more pensive. This was the beginning…what would unfold?

After four and a half hours we approached the town of Uttarkashi, pulling into the Rajaji Hotel on the outskirts of town. It was a welcome sight, perched about 150 meters above the Ganga. The train of Sattva cars all pulled into the parking lot and we rolled out. A little chaos getting checked in, as we would spend the night here, but I was happy that my room was on the same floor as reception and, a bonus…my room was next to Anand-ji, so I would be blessed with his radiance filling the hotel. We all had a typical Indian lunch in the large open restaurant at the hotel. As everywhere the views were stunning…the river, the mountains, the impossibly remote hamlets nestled into the steep slopes.

After lunch, we piled again into our assigned cars for the trip into the Uttarkashi- proper destination: the Kashi Vishwanath temple. While the more famous Kashi Vishwanath temple is in Varanasi, this one stands tall: as the Skanda Purana quotes…Lord Shiva said, "O sages, when the earth is weighed by sins and plagued by demons, the Himalaya will be my abode. Himalaya, which has been blessed from time immemorial, has always been my region in Kali-yuga. The Kashi of the North, Uttarkashi will become exalted as the Kashi of the East (Varanasi) and all other pilgrim centers combined."

The temple itself has the city built up around it and there is a thriving and bustling marketplace, with the usual crush of pilgrims, vendors, scooters and somewhat controlled chaos. We gathered and found our way to the temple grounds, which were quite large. I am still in awe over the manner of worship in the Indian temples. There seems to be so much going on at all times and that was no different here. The women flowing by in their finest saris, shimmering with gold and silver accented highlights, beaming with religious fervor and excitement to be on the temple grounds, always sets the stage for me.

We wandered around the temple grounds for a bit and entered the sacred temple which held the Shiva Linga. The Shiva Linga symbolizes Shiva and is normally in the shape of a stone shaft. Often, it takes a phallic shape, with the ritual three horizontal stripes on it. This one was different and, uniquely, it leans to the south. There is a century old story about why that is, and I didn't uncover it until doing research for this missive. It has to do with the loyalty and devotion of a 16 year old boy for his Lord in Uttarkashi.

We were led through a maze of buildings until we arrived at our own private covered area near the center. We had our own havana (copper fire pit) for the ceremony, which was certainly going to include a yagya, fire ceremony. This we also had for our pilgrimage to Badrinath, although here Sattva had arranged for us to have a priest (turned out to be the High Priest) perform the ceremony. All of us gathered around the havana, the priest took up his spot next to Anand-ji. Note that we were the only group of Westerners on the temple grounds, perhaps in the city. This brought the curious and local faithful to the edge of our space to witness the unusual activity and ceremony.

And it began! Anand-ji, in his impish manner, gave us no indication of what we were about to take part in. The high priest began, and his voice was from another world. I will never forget it. His voice was like a tenor saxophone, and he was talking fast. Very fast. In hindsight, I don't know how he could have spoken less than 30-40,000 words in our hour there. How he memorized it all is a miracle! Of course, all in Sanskrit: mantras prayers and repetitions...we could catch familiar words here and there, but it was hypnotizing. His focus was our Guru Deva, and he had Anand-ji perform numerous rituals with flowers, fire and repetition of verses. He was draped with marigold garlands and was honored as a welcome guest and Guru / Teacher. Throughout the mesmerizing ceremony, the locals were leaning over to watch the spectacle. Towards the end, many wandered into our area and worshipped with our group.

As the ceremony proceeded, I looked around our group to see all our beloved souls enjoying the ceremony. I noticed Tomas and Regina sitting together. They had come up on Tomas' motorcycle, a Royal Enfield Himalaya. I could tell that Regina was being taken up by the spirit of things and going into a samadhi state. She was rocking and nodding, her hands reaching out, going into namaskar, her eyes to the heavens. She is such a beacon of light to all of us, whereby we can see that the higher states are easily available to each one of us.

After an hour or so, the ceremony wound down. We had all received red strings around our wrist from the priest's assistant (as I keypunch, mine is still on my arm). For most of us, I think, we were exhausted spiritually from the hour long ceremony. As the staccato praying and chanting from the high priest came to an end, I saw that Regina had really left for the astral plane. She walked over to Anand-ji and prostrated flat on the ground in front of him. Tears were flowing from her eyes. Generally, our

Guru Deva does not like to have people exhibiting the very normal Hindu actions of kissing their master's feet or lying prostrate. I chalk it up to the fact that a Guru will never say that he is a Guru. He encouraged Regina to her feet, and I was there with Tomas to help steady her. The realm she was in left her in no worldly shape to ride the motorcycle back to the hotel, so I told Tomas I would ride with him and she could ride in the car I came in. He was grateful for the offer. I would sacrifice much for my revered teacher, Tomas, so it was an easy offer.

Tomas is a master bike rider and the ride to the hotel was lovely. Going through the Indian towns on a bike gives you a chance to feel, hear and smell all that is India. It made me think his ride from Sattva to the Rajaji hotel must have been quite exhilarating! Tomas and Regina also motorcycled to Badrinath with us under much colder conditions last year. By the time we got back to the hotel, Regina had returned to the earthly plane. It was quite dark now, so everyone headed off to their rooms for sleep after another magical night in Mother India. Annemarie told us we would be meeting for meditation down at the river at 7AM.

21 OCTOBER 2024

I enjoyed a great sleep; how could it be anything else with my Master sleeping right next door? I got up early and walked down to the river where others had already begun their meditation by the sacred river. I found a rock to sit on and began. When I opened my eyes to sing the Gayatri mantra, I saw Anand-ji perched on a tall rock where he could meditate while overlooking his beloved students and the river. How could a day begin better? I began my normal daily japa practice as we walked back up the hill to the hotel. Sublime.

We all met in the Rajaji Hotel restaurant for breakfast and the energy was high. Today was the day we were arriving in Gangotri, the departure city from which the trail would begin to take us to our ultimate destination…Gaumukh! The headwaters of the Holy Ganga River. Warwick, Bill and I found our driver, who loaded our luggage and found our place in the queue of 14 vehicles, we were car #5, for the five hour drive *DEEP* into the Himalayas. We found conversations coming quite easily and we again covered the waterfront of worldly and Dharmic issues. Of course, the roads become even more twisty and the drop-offs on the sides of the road even more immense.

As we proceeded, we came across an area that was, surprisingly, the apple capital of the northern Himalayas. Plastic apple crates were strewn along the side of the roads and gatherers were harvesting on the steep slopes. Driving along we passed large trucks whose beds were filled with apple crates heading down the mountain to supply the big cities of India with some of Nature's finest. As always, the impossibly small and remote villages and hamlets along the way were visible across the river gorges on the steep mountains. What a lifestyle! All supported by the worship of Shiva. This was Shivalik country and Shiva is the primary god of the vast majority of the peoples in this region. We were traveling 100 km (60 miles) today and it would take us a little over four hours...the going was slow!

From Wikipedia: Gangotri is one of the four sites in the Chota Char Dham pilgrimage circuit It is also the origin of the Ganges river and, per Hinduism, the seat of the goddess Ganga. The source of the Ganges river is the Bhagirathi River, originating from the Gangotri Glacier. Once the river confluences with the Alakananda River at a town called Devprayag it finally acquires the name of Ganga.

Near the river is a stone where King Bhagiratha performed penance to Shiva in order to bring the Ganga down to earth and absolve the sins of his ancestors. According to another legend, Pandavas performed the great 'Deva Yajna' here to atone the deaths of their kinsmen in the epic battle of the Mahabharata. Hindus believe that performing the ancestral rites on the banks of Bhagirathi frees the spirit of the ancestor from the cycle of rebirth and a holy dip in its waters cleanses sins committed in the present also past births.

Warwick (Woz) and Charlotte

Shiva creating the Ganga , at the entrance to Gangotri

Finally, the village of Gangotri started to make its presence known. The cars were slowing, and we all eventually came to a halt. (According to the 2011 Indian census there are 47 families in Gangotri, and the population is 111. I have seen estimates as high as 600, but that is most likely a regional number.) The village cannot accommodate buses, trucks or even our small Dharmic Caravan, so we parked outside the city and walked on in. The porters and drivers would bring our bags. We were now hanging at 3050 meters (10,000 feet) and it was cold, yet sunny. The air was noticeably thinner.

We were directed to the Krishna Restaurant. Of course it was the Krishna Restaurant, what else could it have been! And of course, there was a Mexican portion of the menu...burritos and comida Mexicana in this most remote part of the world! We were really buzzing with excitement now.

The street was lined with many, many vendors selling religious wares and supplies. Also, cold weather and hiking gear. Every stall had the ubiquitous orange plastic bottles, in sizes from small to extra-large. These were used to fill with the holy water of the Ganga headwaters, for use in religious practice at home, put on a home altar, or given to friends as souvenirs. I didn't buy much and ended up handing out dana, alms, to the sadhus. For some reason, I am also the target of those seeking money and I get quickly surrounded. My fellow yogis chuckled at me as I was pressed by the people. Even a blind lady...straight to me in a group of people, her hand out, muttering in her mountain accented tongue.

We had all been given our hotels and room numbers, so it was time to gather up our luggage from the street and "check in". The Sattva staff had reserved a room for each of us depending on our preference, single or double. I was at the Hotel Manisha, one floor walkup. I opened the door, frankly, not knowing what to expect. Nice bed, hot water shower, but no towels, and big blankets for the bed. O Oh! That is when I noticed that there was no heat. Yep. As our Guru Deva says, nothing comes easy and learning always comes with some sort of challenge. As was true the previous night, the bathroom area includes a shower in the same space, everything tiled. No towel and 5 degrees C, (40F), in the room certainly meant a shower was out of the question. I grabbed my heavy North Face parka!

And there was no time for it anyways! We were on our way to the famous aarti at the Gangotri temple. I was astonished by how many people were there. Certainly, far more than there could have been on the trail tomorrow. Just buses and carloads of people arriving at this sacred and holy city to enjoy the aarti and revel in the Himalayan environment. There was nowhere near the number of pilgrims here as there was last October in Badrinath, not even close. But the religious fervor was just as keen, and Shakti filled the thin air. The temple grounds themselves were at the end of the road, literally the end of the road, for beyond was the trail up the valley, into the headwaters of Gaumukh. As always, the Indian women were dressed in their finest saris, and this lent a colorful backdrop to the environment. Gongs were banging and chanting from the temple pujaris filled the air. It was Freezing!

The Holy Temple in Gangotri

We were all seated in front of the temple proper to take in as much as we could. The service proceeded and finally we lined up and worked our way over to the door of the temple proper where the ishta to the goddess Ganga is kept. We were able to peer in, kiss the stoop and offer our prayers. It is said that the goddess descended here when Shiva released the Ganga from the locks of his long flowing hair. The gongs continued, the riot of noise and chanting pervading all.

Turns out the staff had planned a kirtan for us. We were taken to a private room on the perimeter of the square. We left our shoes at the door and entered to sit on the floor. The room was about 5 meters square, and we all huddled in. The musicians began and we all sang along with the songs we know. It went on for some time and then additional local musicians started showing up, as well as a number of townsfolk. The room was jammed, the singing boisterous and the glow of everyone was rosy and bright. It was obvious that all of us foreigners, pilgrims from afar, had created quite a buzz in town, and we were the biggest thing to happen in a long time. When the music wound down, it was clear that a great time was had by all. The lead musician even implored us to "come back tomorrow night"! They were ready for more singing and playing with our festive group! The Sattva people bring joy and bliss wherever we travel! We would have been back, but the 12-mile trail beckoned for tomorrow, and the start of our purposeful adventure.

Back to the Krishna Restaurant for dinner, lots of yakking and continued excitement from the group. Shakti was everywhere and it was getting us pumped up. I meandered back to the hotel and prepared for the next day. I was fully expedition clothed in my hotel room and slept with all my clothes on under those heavy blankets. Sadly, I had to pee in the middle of the night. Oh Shit! OK, make a run for it, T'Om! Couldn't find the light so like a blind man I felt my way along the wall to the bathroom door. Through the window/vent in the bathroom (no dual pane windows at the Manisha Hotel!) I could hear the river rushing past as a reminder of where I was and why I was here. I had my wool, woven slippers on, thankfully, as I am sure my warm feet would have stuck like glue to the frozen floor tile as I made the mad dash to the bathroom and back, praying the cold hadn't invaded my cocoon under the heavy blankets.

THE LONG PATH TO THE HEADWATERS
October 22nd, 2024

Crossing a creek on the Gangotri trail

Surprisingly, I was woken up at 6AM by the bustle of the vendors opening their shoppes and rattling their goods around. That is a pretty early start time for most Indian street vendors, but things do get going very early in Gangotri, as the treks begin early for the long and arduous hike. I had little clue at the time that this day would prove to be one of the most memorable opportunities to rise out of myself that was ever to be.

I reluctantly left the warm bed into the freeze zone of the hotel room. I had prepared everything the night before, when I was fully Arctic Zone dressed before bed. Everything I would need for the 12-mile trek was stuffed into my Addidas day pack and all other necessities: sleeping bag, two more days of clothing, toiletries and misc. trail snacks were crammed into my sixty-liter trekking pack that the porters would take.

I left the room and headed to the Krishna to meet up with the others. It was time. The pilgrimage was to begin after we ate. We all met in the street and were off, hiking down towards the temple where the trail started with 100 or so quite steep steps…just to make sure we were ready for what was ahead! Nothing comes easy in the Dharmic life, despite the bliss and contentment of it all. 100 steps at 10,000 feet gave everyone a good insight into the fact that the air was truly thinner here. I was huffing when the steps met the start of the trail, which was overlooking the town and the temple. As at Badrinath, everyone finds a pace and that usually hooks you up with someone with whom to walk and talk. We didn't get too far when we came to the "official" park ranger station.

At this point, bureaucratic things were moving at a seemingly glacial pace, and the rangers were no exception. Jemina took the docs from everyone and entered the station. Maybe 30 minutes later we were waived through, and the proper beginning was at hand. The trail was a long upward trek, along the river below, that ran through the mountainous valley. As we moved on, the drop off on the side of the trail started to get precipitous. I moved from one pilgrim to another, talking and discussing our lives, why we were here, our history with Sattva and making new friends from all over the world once more. We passed very few people who were coming down, and I don't think anyone passed us going up. They permit only around 100 people on the trail on any given day.

There were various breaks along the way and the group spread out a considerable amount. I found myself in the last third. I am always OK with that as, at 72 years of age, I am always the grandpa on these excursions. After about four hours we came to a wooded area (much of the hike was above the tree line) and it was time for a 30 minute break and lunch. I had plenty of trail snacks, but I wasn't hungry, while I was tired as hell. I found a spot on the outside of the gathered group and flopped down and took a nap under a bush! I probably wasn't drinking enough water, which has been my MO for decades as a runner, so didn't think much of it. It was also clear that there were some people who were having a tough time with the elevation. I was one of them! I was fit and ready, but the thin air and lack of oxygen was obviously getting to me a bit, sapping my strength.

When I woke up Anand-ji told me he never takes naps, but I inspired him to take a short one! Ma Ganga, I inspired my Guru Deva! Already things to be grateful for. While the trail was not arduous, it did continue up and up, despite some downhill spots to cross the various streams and creeks coming down from the peaks all around us, feeding the river below. Crossing some of those was interesting to see how locals had made bridges over the streams...they seemed made of thin branches that couldn't hold us, but the nature on the mountain is mighty, and no one fell through.

I didn't have my journal in hand, and it now is very clear to me that I cannot recall many of the conversations I had on the way up. Things seemed to be getting a little wonky. We all pressed on, walking higher and higher into the thinner air. I stopped a lot, trying to listen to my body. Of course, my ego wanted to press on with those at the front of the pack, but my legs and lungs said no. So, I just chilled and put one foot in front of the next. The path was all things Himalayan...rocky at points, with both pebbles and larger boulders for the way forward. Much of the time there were steep drop-offs. On occasion there were areas where one was walking on big rocks, and the trail became a bit hard to follow.

At this point, however, it became abundantly clear to me that I had entered the arena of having a pilgrimage into T'Om. While not exactly like climbing Everest, my every step was thought about and exercised with attention. My intention was going inward, while my body was going up and on. Who are you? Where are you? What brought you here, to this moment? Is this really T'Om, living his dreams, trekking the Himalayas with his fellow yogis and his Guru Deva? How did this happen? Was I on the wings of Garuda?

I was, almost with knowing it, becoming a Shaivas, a follower of Shiva. I came into Sattva two years ago as a Hanuman guy as that was the primary deity of my Tucson Guru, Hari Rai Khalsa. Her depth of love for him was contagious and he is so easy to revere, with that open, bhakti heart. Of course, at my age, I needed the Hanumanic strength on a daily basis, especially when surrounded by so many strong and fit yogis in their 20s, 30's and 40's! But what to do? Anand-ji's guy is Shiva and it is impossible not to be drawn into that divine world of this all-pervading deity when at Sattva. And the entire region around northern India here, and the Himalayas, was Shiva country.

So, while I have always felt that Sri Hanuman has helped push me to new heights, here in the Shilvalik mountains, the presence and power of Shiva is all pervading. And he was the one! The one who gifted Mother India with the Ganga, here in his own majestic mountains. Out of his flowing dreadlocked hair, from his airy abode, he released the Ganga to the world.

The path was always up, maybe gently sometimes, but up.

I could feel him...actually, he was laughing at me. Knowing I was working my ass off to be in his realm. Making real the spiritual fact that no growth comes without effort. No transcendence happens without grappling with one thing or another. He gifted me with a cake walk at the other end of his realm in Badrinath, but Gaumukh was another cup of sacred Indian tea! I started out thinking I was in control of this sacred trek and would be pulled along the eleven mile hike and 2500 feet of elevation climb, holding hands and gaily laughing with Lord Ganesha who would, in the flick of a trunk, remove all obstacles for me.

I now know I am not in charge, and I wrote a book about it! But here, in the now, it has become so real. It doesn't mean I can float in the canoe of life, with no concern or effort, down the Dharmic river of life. Or that my path has been divinely laid out and all I need to do is relax and enjoy. Non, au contraire! There is effort to be exhibited, and that effort will result in evolving, it will result in the path becoming wider and more easily understood and adhered to.

And right there and now, the journey became a metaphor for understanding the daily work that needs to be done to open the doors that have been held for us by the teachers, masters and gurus through the millennia. And right there and right now, I questioned if I was up to the task on this brilliant blue day, in these sacred mountains. I noticed that I was the last person from our group on the trail, with everyone else ahead of me! What! I pulled up to the final group resting area, about 2 kilometers from base camp. I found a rock to sit on and dropped my day pack to the ground to get water and an energy bar. To rest and breathe. Ecstasy!

I wasn't there but a couple of minutes and Anand-ji moseyed on over to give me a good look in the eye. "Are you doing all right? How are you feeling?" Not wanting to fail at being up to the task, I cheerily told him I was AOK, just listening to my body, taking my time. Like all Sattva people, we never know if Anand-ji is reading our mind, especially when his deep brown eyes stare into yours. I really just kind of hoped that I could kid him, and he would say, OK, fine, take it slow. Be mindful. Ha! No such luck!

He kept staring into my eyes and gaining a consensus of my situation. He said, "Your lips are blue." I never expected him to say that, unless perhaps he had taken me to such heights that I was manifesting Krishna or Shiva! I was busted. It was a sure sign that I was feeling the effects of altitude sickness. He called over Pennie, an absolutely inspiring yogi of the highest degree, who was traveling with us as the nurse, she being an RN, from Alabama, who spent much time in India leading retreats of her own and at Sattva for the holy knowledge.

Pennie pulled an oximeter out of her bag and put it on my finger. (Remember that the last song on the radio before I left Tucson was "Penny Lover" ...that is typical Sattva synchronicity!) Of course, it reflected a lower state of oxygen than was normal...96-98 is normal, mine was 82. Somehow the oximeter was also able to give her a blood pressure reading and it was also not up to snuff. Crap! What now?

Anand-ji said, "Have you been drinking enough water? More than enough?"   The answer was no. As mentioned, 40 years of running brought me to the understanding that my body didn't require hydrating as is the current fashion. I could easily find fluids stored in my body to satisfy my nourishment needs. I never ever carried a water bottle. Much of my running was done in the tropics, where I lived in Hawaii for 16 years, and Huntington Beach, California for 25 years. One thing both of those locales have in common is they are both at sea level elevation. I found myself today at 12,000 feet of elevation and things were different, apparently.

At this point Anand-ji told the rest of the group to continue on and that he was going to stay behind a bit to attend to me. And this, dear readers, turned out to be my gift from my Guru Deva.

One I will never forget. One that will be seared into my consciousness for the rest of my life and perhaps longer...

And we started to continue our walk. Anand-ji said, "OK, here is what we are going to do. I am going to walk in front of you to set the pace. I am going to tell you how to breath and we are going to walk one step per breath at a time." The first directive was. "Three parts in through the nose, one part out through the mouth for each step." And we began. I was blessed to have Pennie following me and the owner of the trekking company walking next to me so that I wouldn't have a misstep and slide off the side of the mountain. If Anand-ji heard me miss a breath, he would stop, wait for me to get my rhythm, and begin again.

I am not sure how far this foursome walked or how long it took. I am thinking maybe 2 kilometers and about an hour. My body felt heavy. Of course, I was crestfallen and beyond embarrassed. I couldn't understand how this was happening. It didn't manifest in the Badrinath Pilgrimage and that was a steeper climb, but only 5km vs the 18 km we were doing today. I worried that I hadn't been strident enough in my asana practice or maybe it was due to the extra 7 or 8 kilos I was carrying around in body fat.

As we walked it soaked in that this was nothing to be embarrassed about, this was just what had been set out for me. This was my challenge, quite a supreme one, and who was there to stand by my side and help me through it...none other than my Guru Deva. I took the opportunity to do that which all of his students yearn to do...I had a long and lengthy conversation with him. Mano a mano. I spoke to him about becoming a father (his wife was due in 5 weeks with their first child), express my delight in the new shrine area on Campus, about the gift he gives in the time and energy of teaching the ancient wisdom. I spoke to him about my hopes and dreams for a possible upcoming motorcycle pilgrimage. I expressed gratitude for the Grace that brought me to Sattva and changed my life forever.

We walked on and on. I never got a sense of frustration (from him or Pennie) about the slow pace. We rounded a corner on the trail and, magically, before us was the base camp, with tents, Quonset huts and domed spaces that would be our home for the next two nights. The river was rushing alongside and the snow covered, deep Himalayas lay before us and on each side. Even through my mists, I could tell we had arrived at a vortex. A spiritual center on the blue planet. We walked downhill to the site and entered the dome building which would be our gathering place and eating house. All the other pilgrims were waiting in a seated circle looking at us as we arrived.

Our home base in Gaumukh, the river running alongside

I spoke. "Thank you all for your prayers and well wishes. They were so well received. I am here with you now. The message I would like to share with you is what you have all just witnessed. Our Guru Deva will not forsake you. He will be with you, at your side, even in your most challenging moments. Count on him. Depend on him. He will not forsake you." There was silence as that soaked in. Pennie went to get me some hot tea and refilled my cup often. She wanted to warm up my core.

I encourage all readers visit to Google maps, entering Gangotri, India and then click directions to Gaumukh. Put it on satellite view and take a look at the trek. Then back out the map, way out, and look at where all of us pilgrims found ourselves. You begin to get an idea of how far into nature's wonder we were. How could this be? How could we be in this remote space? Coming from all over the world as we had. It was not by accident, but through divine direction, that we had all come to this spot. Led by our master.

Of course, everyone was bushed. The staff assigned tents and brought our duffels to each one. I climbed in and began to organize my 40 sq feet of real estate in holy Gaumukh. It was slow! I was moving glacially. First the foam mat, then the sleeping bag. Then get my meds and toiletries sorted. Arrange my clothes for the night and the next day. I was not hungry, didn't really know what I was. But dinner was soon to be served, and we all found our way back to the dome.

As soon as the sun descended beyond the mighty Himalayas, it got cold fast! I was completely pooped, as was everybody, and ready to sleep. I arranged everything a little more and climbed into my bag. I used my clothes from the hike up, rolled up, to make a pillow. My socks were on, flannel shirt and pajama bottoms. I fell asleep fast and woke up about three hours later and had to pee, the downside of all that hydrating. I was shivering up a storm. Unzip the tent and wander out, looking for the nearest big bush. I looked up! Sweet Lord, I have never seen anything like it. With no ambient light, literally none, interfering with the darkness of the skies, the stars were ablaze. The Milky Way, shimmering stars and planets, it was impressive and a sight that was by itself worth the trip.

I am sure it was 12 F or -11C out there and I would not warm up again for the rest of the night. Tossing and turning, waking up every 60 to 90 minutes. Literally shaking in my socks. I was not ready for this, much to my dismay. Dawn came and as always on this pilgrimage, we were all off to the river to meditate. Some of my more devoted travelers were wading in the river, some bathing…for sure it was right at freezing in the water. As always, it is such bliss to settle in with a group of meditators. Especially high in the Shivalik range here. After 30 minutes, opening eyes and seeing a larger group assembled, all looking for inner peace and quiet through the meditative process.

Morning at the Side of Ma Ganga

23 October, 2024

Magic, as a Himalayan raven landed on Anand-ji's hand.

The staff served a warm organic vegetarian breakfast, lots of hot tea and a surprise, some of the delicious mountain apples. Anand-ji said that there would be another trek, continuing up another 500 feet to a sacred spot overlooking the glacier. I had not recovered my lungs yet, so I stayed behind with a couple of the other folks still suffering from altitude sickness. As it turned out, some magic happened on that second hike, that I sadly missed. Anand-ji was standing on a rock talking to those assembled and had his arms outspread. And like that a Himalayan crow landed on his hand...and stayed there. These hearty birds are only found in Gangotri / Gaumukh and Badrinath, the sacred mountain homes of Shiva.

I just sat around camp and took in the vistas of deep blue skies, snowcapped mountains and the sounds of the river. Here I was, in the seat of the headwaters of the Ganga River. The holy river that feeds, shelters and give spiritual upliftment to millions and millions of Hindus and Indian people. Even in late fall, the river was rushing loudly and with force. There was a hand operated bridge across that had a hot air balloon type basket attached to it. People would climb in and with great effort, pull themselves to the other side of the river so that that could continue hiking deeper into the range. It was often quite comical as it was about 150 meters across, and everyone had various methods of getting to the other side.

And yet, here I was, a man originally from Michigan, in the middle of the USA, about as far from home as I could possibly get. What are the forces of the Divine that brought me here and planted me alongside the Ganga at 3500 meters in elevation? At my age, at my state of spiritual development, at my fitness level? Only the omniscience of the Divine could have arranged this. It was impossible to conceive in any other light than that. Prior to my 300 hour Yoga teacher training, sitting with my Tucson Guru, I told her, "Hari Rai, I am giving it my all. I am not holding back. I am going to accept each and everything the Cosmic Consciousness puts before me. I am going with my wings spread wide open, ready to receive and ready to trust. Trust in the knowledge, trust in my Inner Guru, trust in the Brahman All."

And that has not changed. It is exactly my intent and attitude every single time I head to Mother India. I am here for a reason. I have been guided here, the pull is unmistakable, and I will dive in and accept it all to the greatest of my ability. This bhakti has never, ever let me down. Au contraire, it has only always filled my heart with love and compassion, grown my spirit to high heights and blessed my every waking moment with what to me is the greatest of all gifts in my life...gratitude for the grace in my life that has put me at the foot of all off this wonder.

I have learned that we are not the created, but we are the Creator of our lives. Every single thing that happens unfolds according to the plan that we have knowingly or unknowingly laid out. We are the God of our Universe. It is found within and from listening to the Inner Voice we can find liberation. We can free ourselves from all our attachments, physical or material, and live the lives that we are striving for.

As I sit along this sacred river, these thoughts are flooding in, and I know I am right where I need to be. In the last 30 months I have found myself, I have found God, I have found Love, peace and contentment like never before in my life. It is clear that I am not on this spot on the top of the world by accident. I imagined that since I first had the experience of seeing God, an LSD assisted samadhi 55 years ago, that I am on the path, however I wavered and wondered, that led to this moment. I would NEVER turn back. And I never shall. Anand-ji talks repeatedly about how it is through challenge, work and effort that the world opens up to us. It is the key to evolving, transcending and growth. And that right there is what Mother Nature wants from us. Every day! Grow and evolve.

And this is why we meditate, do our japa, attend puja, aarti, perform yagya. Practice yoga asana and kriya. Why we study and read sacred passages, books, listen to kirtan and sacred music from Deva Premal and Krisha Das. It is all our Dharmic job, our joyful work. It has become apparent to me and so many other hundreds of Sattva students that this work pays manifold dividends, the greatest of which is that each and every day we see the path widening, we see the great spiritual mysteries come into clarity and the following of that very path becomes easier and easier every day.

And I never plan to stop, will never cease to grow, will never wither away into the habit energy that says, "Cut it out, relax, you are working too hard. Just sit back in your recliner and watch TV, let the world go by, go to the bar and have a few drinks, act like everyone else." Yes, the joyful work will continue. The serene bliss that comes from listening to my Guru Deva speak about beauty of the spiritual world, the joy that comes from finishing my seventh yoga practice of the week and the happiness that I receive in just sitting down and writing these books.

As the pilgrimage to T'Om continues, all this beautiful energy is raining down upon my being. It is seating itself in my Atman. I have found my place. I have found my Guru, I have found my Divine Within. And looking out at the world, seeing 8 billion people walking around on this Blue Planet. Knowing that each one of them has the same Divine Within, that they are part of my family, and I have the highest expectation for all of them.

The morning trek is over and now Anand-ji has said that he will give a talk outside in the gorgeous sunlit area in front of one of the very few buildings at the base camp.

(The notes from this talk were taken on a digital recorder, which was lost in the baggage nightmare surrounding the next pilgrimage.)

Dinner comes and goes. I want to be with my beloveds and resist the desire to retire to the tent. There are a few of us in the dome, talking about life. There is an Israeli living in Australia, Eran, who traveled with his wife Ritika, a teacher at Sattva and fellow AMS (altitude mountain sickness) sufferer, and Marouf, a Palestinian man. I am fascinated as these two men reach across the great divide that has separated them for centuries. I am getting a lesson in geopolitics and religion and seeing firsthand how two people from completely opposite camps, truly at war with each other, can come to have a meaningful, deep and lengthy discussion about the situation. I shall never forget it. Big Men, Holy Men, Men searching for peace, forgiveness and a solution. They hugged each other after the 90 minute talk. The divide was breached. There is hope, light and love in the world if we can just talk, put aside our attachments, and open our hearts. This is the way to go to bed, learning, living and growing.

I was ready tonight! I put on 4 pairs of socks, two pair of flannel pajama bottoms and two sweatpant bottoms, 2 long sleeved tee shirts, a sweatshirt, a flannel shirt and then my big and bulky North Face parka. I wrapped a scarf around my neck and put on a Himalayan wool cap. I must have looked like the Michelin man as I tried to wiggle and squeeze all of that and me into my tent and sleeping bag. But I stayed warm, and I slept as well as could be expected; on the ground, in the sub-freezing air 12,500 feet above sea level, under the Himalayan stars, alongside Ma Ganga.

TREK BACK TO GANGOTRI

25 OCTOBER 2024

As Cat Stevens said, "Morning has broken" and it did so with brilliance, with the joy and expectation of a new day. Departure day. I was feeling a bit better and ready for the trek back to Gangotri. Everything packed up and handed over to the porters, typical Indian breakfast and we were off. It was about a 200 foot elevation rise out of the bowl the base camp was in and I found myself huffing and puffing. Nothing would stop me now, though. I was heading down, into thicker air, I was ready. I had wonderful discussions throughout the day. An English gentlemen who was on the walk with his wife. An Indian guy, Sameer, living in London, who was a private banking consultant with Goldman Sachs. My beloved Elena, my esteemed teachers from Sattva-St. Karen, Jemina, Annemarie, Charlotte, radiant Pennie, Alice-who I teamed up with often at masters training and many others.

The eleven miles out seemed slightly less challenging than the eleven in. I was hydrating, eating snacks-loved those dried mangos, and being mindful. I was still in the last 10% contingent, but I could have cared less. I was going to finish on my own two feet. I think it was about seven hours back to Gangotri. I was spent! Kinda of wandering side to side on the trail. But there in the distance was the temple and the end of the hike was in view. I managed to walk right past the area with 100 steps up to the trail and found myself wandering in the residential area of the small village. Of course, all the homes are on the side of the mountain and there are steps and slopes. I managed to find my way down to the main road and stumbled onto a stoop next to a sadhu, who took one look at me and said, "Welcome brother, sit and rest...be with us." I enjoyed his company until another one of our group wandered by and I fell into his shadow and made my way to, where else? The Krishna Restaurant! Hare Krishna!

The group wandered to the entrance of the town where we assembled to prepare for departure. The drivers rounded up the cars and after about an hour everything was packed in and we were ready for the return trip. It was a reasonably quiet four hour drive back to the Rajaji hotel in Uttarkashi. I had the same room, adjacent to the radiance coming from Anand-ji's room next door and slept like a rock after a hearty meal. The heat in the room, the nice shower, it really was a delight.

MUSINGS ON THE RETURN TO SATTVA

25 OCTOBER, 2024

We woke up for meditation down at the river and then a wisdom talk from Anand-ji in a hotel open area. There was breakfast and off we zoomed again. Down, down, down from the high villages, into the Rishikesh city life. Along the way there was an incredibly long (scores of kilometers) reservoir, nestled in the valley between the mountains. It was simply beautiful. Spending warm Indian days along the shores there, taking in the Hindu spirit and reveling in Ma Nature sounded like a great vacation and I filed it away.

Fall is the smog time in northern India and as we dropped in elevation, the push of Delhi's smog started to show a brown smudge in the air. And soon enough the vistas were gone and the city was upon us. Traffic and people walking everywhere. Street vendors, motorcycles, scooters and bicycles. We plowed into the middle of the city and pushed our way to the outskirts on the other side, crossing the Ganga and entering the rural road that led 20 more kilometers to Sattva. Soon we all fell out of our cars and made our way into the café for a late lunch at about 14:00. I managed a nap, then a yoga practice in Shakti Hall. The afternoon and evening were left to our thoughts

The following day started with puja and meditation. I was thrilled when Charlotte led the journey as that rounded out the day with sublime grace. I had a full Sattva breakfast, and we went into a wisdom talk with Anand-ji in Shiva Hall. Ever loving to tease me, he right off the bat commented, "Nice socks, T'Om!" I told him that they were the homemade socks that

Uma had handed out prior to the Badrinath Pilgrimage. My feet are always cold, so I often wear them around. I even bought 10 pairs in Rishikesh to hand out for Christmas gifts when I returned home.

It was off to lunch at Avenue 18 with Elena in prep for our going away celebration that Sattva was giving us. After lunch, I initiated Elena into Kriya 2 in a lovely private ceremony, took a big nap and got ready to party…Sattva Style. Anand-ji has some favorite Indian musicians he often has up from Haridwar, and they really bring it. Maybe four songs over 90 minutes total…Shiva Shiva Shiva Shambo (one of my all- time favorites, eternally etched in my mind when our post-Masters driver to Delhi played the song for 6 hours straight as Silvi, Courtney and I enjoyed being blissed out passengers). Of course, Om Namah Shiviah was a well-loved tune. Anand-ji and many people were dancing and laughing. I crashed hard that night with thoughts swirling from Anand-ji's wisdom talk earlier in the day.

Elena from Manitoba, Canada, was also in my 200 hour class

Waking up to a beautiful blue-sky day for puja and meditation and rolling into a Journey from Anand-ji. We knew right away that it would be deep, as the kriyas were coming fast and furious. He took us away to places only he can access and share and then moved into his famous four sets of ten chaturangas. Dripping wet with sweat what would be next but partner work!

The journey was 100 minutes and ended in a big circle with everyone looking around, eye-gazing.

My beloved Pennie told me a bit later that I had made an impact in her life, walking the Gangotri trail together. As always, synchronicity is at play as I wanted to tell her the same thing that morning, about how much grace and compassion she had shared and how deeply meaningful it was for me and still is to this day.

There was wisdom talk later. These are so divine after our Guru Deva has been on pilgrimage. His spirit is soaring, and he brings an abundance of the holy mountains into his Cosmic Consciousness, opening up to receive all they have to offer. Thereafter, Annemarie announced that we would be going to dinner at the Rasa Hotel, across the river. She is such a kidder! About an hour earlier I had asked her if we would be going over there, as we had done after the Badrinath Pilgrimage!

That evening we all shuttled into Rishikesh for an aarti on the Ganga. The location is just down the steps to the river from Anand-ji's childhood home. He tells us that many, many times he has sat in this spot with his teacher, Maha-ji, to learn, pray and just be in his presence. The pundit had prepared the banana leaf bowls with flowers and a candle, and we all floated ours in the river sending of cares and tensions into the flow of the Holy Ganga. Aartis were simultaneously happening all up and down the river and it was a festive and sacred scene. It is one of the scared rituals in India that just draw you in and confirm that you are, indeed, in Mother India.

Jemina, Nena and Charlotte at the aarti on the Ganga

Back at Sattva, Anand-ji announced that, "We are ready to go the Rasa and everyone should thank T'Om, as he has requested this." He gets such a kick out of putting me in the spotlight and joking around with me. And truly, vice versa. At the 300 hour teacher training graduation, we received our diplomas one by one, hugged our teachers and walked over to Anand-ji, to get / give a Big Hug with our Master, sharing a few words. Mine for him were, "You have done a wonderful job here, with Sattva and with your life. Young Man, and I am very proud of you!" Later I told his wife my remarks and she said, "Oh, he will love that!" Of course, I am 30 years older than he, so calling him young man, is appropriate, while simply crazy. He is an ancient one, with his understanding, omniscient heart!

The next morning Jemina told me that Anand-ji wanted to see me in his office! Oh, dream of dreams. A one on one with my teacher, my master, my Guru Deva. It was sublime. On our trek, I felt like we had truly sealed out relationship, and at this final meeting our eternal friendship was in fact, sealed permanently. Most of the chat was deeply personal and spiritual, but he did tell me how happy he was I was getting married and offered to officiate the wedding…if I could get Kathleen to Rishikesh! Well, no chance of that as she inhabits the North pole of our relationship and me, the South Pole. India is off the books for her, as much as she acknowledges the light my "other home" has brought into our lives. It helps us meet in the equator and tropics of life, which is just fine for me.

That talk rounded out my pilgrimage in a manner of Sat, Chit , Ananda. I felt like I had it all now and truly a part of the Sattva family, not just hoping or dreaming about it happening someday.

BACK TO TUCSON FOR JOY AND BLISS

Kathy and Koko, on her 13th birthday, with a Special doggy birthday cake!

It was get-away day, time to begin the integration from the adventure at the headwaters of the Ganga. As always, the trip home, completing another around the world journey, was flawless and without incident. 30 hours later I was deplaning at Tucson International, heading to the curb and the loving arms (and paws) of Kathleen and Koko.

The next night was the Big Night! Kathy had no idea why I asked her to make a reservation at a better restaurant in town Normally I would wany to stay home for two or three days and completely decompress with my hot tub, her love and comfort food. We were enjoying our sumptuous Italian meal out when I moved my chair aside and kneeled down to the floor, on one knee. She absolutely did not know what was happening as she had resolved in her heart that T'Om was never going to ask her to marry him. She didn't believe it, encouraged me to get in my chair, that people were looking. When I stayed put and assured her that I did want to marry her and truly seal up our love, her radiant joy filled my heart. I was grateful for Anand-ji and all the training that had opened my heart, healed me of my pain from my past marriage and gave me the courage and knowledge that this was part of my path to Unity, my journey and my liberation.

About 7 weeks after returning home, the email came! "You have been invited to participate in the third and final motorcycle tour to the highest roads in the Himalayas with Anand-ji, in September of 2025." That was it! Top of the bucket list, absolute peak! I sent in my deposit and began my spiritual, physical and heart felt preparations for 18 days with my Guru….

WHEELS OF AWAKENING

OUR MOTORCYCLE PILGRIMAGE INTO THE HIMALAYAN REGION OF LADAKH, INDIA

IT BEGINS AGAIN

MA INDIA BECKONS FOR THE SEVENTH TIME

Ok, It is January 4th, 2025. The holidays festivities are in the rear-view mirror now and the mission is implementing the New Year's resolutions. I have three…BYD. That is Book, Yoga, Diet.

Book. I have not been putting the kind of effort into my Gangotri pilgrimage Book that had need to. Kick it up before the memory fades…the integration of the experience never will and shall always remain within me.

Yoga. I worked hard prior to departure last October on my asana. Not as hard as for the Badrinath pilgrimage the year prior, but I stayed at it. Gangotri took it out of me though and upon return, my practice dwindled almost nothing. Now it is going to be every morning with SattvaConnect after meditation.

Diet. One of the reasons I was so challenged on the Gangotri pilgrimage, including a nice visit from altitude sickness, was the simple fact that I had put on 6 or 7 kilos. For me, it doesn't feel good, it is uncomfortable and I feel like I am letting myself down by not fostering an appropriate amount of self-control.

Anyways, as I have every morning since my first 200 hour yoga teacher training class at Sattva, I sat down to meditate after waking up around 5:30 or so. I always have a glass of iced tea (very difficult to do in Ayurvedic India, where iced beverages are a no go). I take a quick minute to check emails before starting… and THERE IT WAS! The announcement I had been waiting for…before ever meeting Anand-ji or going to India for training.

The email delivered the news that a final Motorcycle Tour in the Himalayas with my Guru Deva was being organized. This is what was sent...

ON THE ROAD AGAIN!

Wheels of Awakening - The Ride We've All Been Waiting For!

It's happening! After endless requests and overwhelming demands, Anand Ji is back on the road for one final Moto bike adventure!

Some experiences are so profound, they shape the course of our lives. This is one of those rare moments. This is not just a trip, it's an inner pilgrimage, a call to awaken, and a journey that will never happen again.

Introducing "Wheels of Awakening" a soul-stirring adventure that promises to take you beyond the roads and into the depths of your being. This is your last chance to ride alongside Anand Ji.

It's the last ride, a legendary experience that is all about freedom, awakening, and connection to yourself, to the community, and to the vast, untamed beauty of the Himalayas.

This final Moto pilgrimage is reserved only for the sincere seekers, those who feel the pull to explore not only the roads but also the depths of their own being.

Open to both riders and passengers. Even if you don't ride, you can still join this legendary experience as a passenger and immerse yourself in the wisdom and stillness of the Himalayas.

So, are you ready to hit the road with Anand Ji? Don't let this chance pass you by — because once it's gone, it's gone. Reserve Your Spot Now. Let's make this final ride the most unforgettable one yet. We're saving a spot just for you. endless

With love and light, The Sattva Family

I read it three times. Out of the blue...my dream! I mean, after all, this is how I found Anand-ji...wandering through the Gaia Network looking for some spiritual / alternative entertainment. And there it was! A young Indian Guru taking his students on a motorcycle tour high in the Himalayas, "The Highest Pass." There were ten episodes of this epic journey and by the third one, I knew if I went to India to take teacher training, it would be at Sattva, from Mr. Anand Mehrotra. The movie changed my life and set me on a Yogic path that would bring me to India six times in forty months. I recounted the first two years in my book, "*Living Fearless*".

My mind was spinning and going into overdrive. At Last! The opportunity I had been waiting for. I folded my legs into seated easy pose, put my right hand up to my forehead and began Nadi Shoshana, the ancient Kriya practice using alternative nostril breathing to balance the brain in preparation for meditation. Then hands down for Kriya 2, a most sacred Kriya that settles the mind and begins with focused, correct thought. And then I started the central part of meditation, my mantra. Normally, I am shortly zoomed away into meditative thought, but it just wasn't happening right off the bat today. All I could think about was the ride, my dream. Would I use miles or pay for the ticket? Would Kathy be OK with another 3+ week trip? I am going to have to buy some leather chaps, a leather jacket, heavy boots and a helmet. And on and on. I ended up dropping in, but it took focus and resolve.

I responded to the online request to participate immediately after meditation and headed downstairs to my yoga room to enjoy a class taught by St. Karen on SattvaConnect. This was all part of the New year's routine now. Meditation, then straight down for yoga practice. How I love SattvaConnect! Here I can take classes from my beloved teachers in Rishikesh on demand, St Karen, Tomas, Annemarie, Charlotte and, of course, Anand-ji. I moved through St. Karen's class with joy in my heart...both for being in my practice again and the hoped for upcoming trip! When I had finished up, I whistled for Koko, my beloved golden retriever, to come down so we could go on our morning 2km walk. This was the time when I did my japa practice, each and every day, with Koko alongside. My current japa mantra was "Om Namo Guru Dev Namo"...*I will listen to the Divine voice from within and heed it throughout the day. I will acknowledge the Guru within and let that true self always manifest itself in my being.* Six 108 bead rounds of the mala, the mantra repeated 648 times.

We returned home and I immediately whipped up an e-mail to Badoni, the magician who manages to herd all the yogi cats, their travel needs and the many responsibilities and organizational skills that revolve around the Sattva Yoga Academy. I told him I wanted to make sure my application had been received, as I submitted it on my phone, in the dark. I told him my dream had come true, and that Anand-ji had told me on a couple of occasions that I would be invited to the next motorcycle adventure. I was pulling out all the stops. I reminded him that after our Badrinath pilgrimage, I joined Anand-ji and eight others on a motorcycle day tour out of Sattva. He knew I could ride! Badoni responded the next day that my request had been duly recorded and that I was placed on the docket!

After breakfast, I broke the news to Kathy, now my fiancée (I call her my Beyonce!), about the trip. She knew where this experience lived in my heart. And even though it scared the heck out of her, she had come to know how deeply each visit to India affected me and the complete bliss with which I returned with after each India trp. She shrugged her shoulders knowing that her support was essential to the trip and there was little to stop me from my dream.

I dove into my computer, doing hours and hours of research finding the best fares or the best frequent flyer mile deals. I got it sorted out, everything was within reach, and I stopped. I was not going to follow through and do all the finish work of booking without confirmation that it was a go for me to join the trip. O please, all the gods, hear my plea! May this journey be the path that you have set out for me as you continue to open doors in the spiritual realm that I have come to love.

ACCEPTANCE

January 6th, 2025. 6AM

Oh, Sweet Lord! As I am sitting down for my meditation... there it is! An email from Badoni! Could it be? Already? I slowly opened it and...***IT IS!!!!!*** I have been extended an official invitation to be on the ride! While Master Yogi that I am, my meditation was trashed! My excitement level was at an all-time high, my mind reeling and I was jumping out of my seat. When the alarm went off, ending meditation, I was so blissed out that I completely skipped my six closing Gayatri mantras!

Bang!, straight to my desktop computer where I researched and found some great flights and fares. August 30th, 2025, Tucson to Delhi, premium economy seats, 48,000 miles. September 19th, 2025, Delhi to Tucson, business class, 70,000 miles! For traveling halfway around the world, those were some pretty great fares! Not only were they great, they were far and away the best Delhi round trip fares I had ever had. The stars were aligning! I was locked in! The journey was laid out for me, I just had to follow through, listen and submit to what will be.

In the welcome letter, there was a list containing information on what would be provided on the trip and some details. I was surprised that the journey would include a round-trip flight from Dehradun, the closest city to Rishikesh with an airport, to Leh, India, deep in the Himalayas. I typed Leh into Google maps and saw that it was 3500 meters (11,500 feet) in elevation, in the Ladakh region. In Ladakh there are 25 named mountains, of which Saltoro Kangri is the highest at 7700 meters (25,000 feet). This is the scared region into which my Guru Deva is taking us...the Abode of the Gods...on motorcycles!

I also noted that the distance driving from Rishikesh to Leh was 900 km (560 miles). The airplane trip would certainly give us a head start and plant us deep into the sacred mountains. I would much rather put the butt time in an airplane seat to deep in the mountains than on an overly long bike drive up there. We would get in more than enough miles on the pilgrimage.

I realized immediately that I needed to do some deep research and digging on Acute Mountain Sickness (AMS) which happens at high altitudes from the lack of oxygen in the air. I had gotten it on our trek to the headwaters of the Ganga River near Gangotri in November 2024, where the symptoms manifested themselves at about 11,500 feet! Our base camp (hotel) in Leh for this trip was the same 11.500 feet.

My AMS was scary stuff, although I was a bit too out of it to realize that at the time. It slowed me down to being the last of our group of 40 in the hiking line. We had a nurse along on the trip and she confirmed my symptoms. As it unfolded, Anand-ji sent the rest of the group ahead to the camp and he, Pennie and the head guy from the trekking company, slowly walked, step by step with me to the camp about 2 km away. Step by step, Anand-ji in front of me giving me breathing instructions culled from our Kriyas. Cosmic breathing! He wanted to hear it, or he would stop, wait and resume after I got in rhythm again. I have no recollection of how long it took, but I learned right then and there, that even in the middle of this sacred pilgrimage, my Guru did not forsake me. Pennie was making sure I was hydrating and the guide walked alongside of me so I didn't slip and topple hundreds of feet down into the gorge.

That night I tossed and turned. Could I do this? Was this going to be too high for me? We would be riding to over 18,000 feet. Would I have to cancel even before I started? I fell asleep saying Om Namah Shiviah, over and over again.

In meditation the next morning it became clear to me that of course I could do this. I had gotten AMS 15 km into an 18 km uphill mountain hike. In September I would be on a motorcycle, exerting virtually no energy at all. And this trip was my destiny. Everything in the last 25 years of my life that had been happening was pointing to this very moment in the Himalayas. And then it clearly came to me that I had written a book called "Living Fearless". The foundation of that book is that our life is already laid out for us, everything moves forward in a manner that manifests the divine, and to acknowledge that means I really have no reason for any fear. The Brahman All is in charge at all times and if one just allows life and the cosmic consciousness to run the show, only what is supposed to happen will happen. And in my life, that has all been flowing upward to the divine.

Yes, there will be challenges on the trip. No, it will not be a bed of roses. There is no growth without some work, some mountains to climb, some effort to be exerted. There will be questioning, there will be cold, there will be complications. But this pilgrimage on two wheels to the highest temples in the world will also be a pilgrimage into myself. The trek to Gangotri proved that clearly. Can I meet the challenges that the universe puts before me in order to evolve and transcend as it wants for me? Of course I can. I have done it for my whole life. Stay in the Flow!

It was quite apparent that I needed to prepare and prepare like I had never prepared for anything before. I had nine months to do so. And it started, even though I didn't know it at the time, one week ago. With my New Year's resolutions. Back to asana, attention to diet and nutrition, focus and study incredible Hindu knowledge that Anand-ji had bought forth. And Kriya. Breath exercise and practice. I have been taught over 200 Kriya exercises and all of them will come in handy as I give my lungs every opportunity to be strong and supportive.

I Googled altitude sickness. That led to a deep dive. I discovered there are a couple of medicines that can help forestall AMS. Diamox surfaced as the most prevalent and I will be talking to my doctor and cardiologist about those in the coming months. (I subsequently received the Diamox prescription, with more than enough additional pills to help anyone who finds themselves suffering AMS like I did.)

It was funny, looking back at the Badrinath pilgrimage almost two years prior. We went to similar heights and even though I felt the actual trek was more difficult and strenuous, I had no effects of AMS at all. What changed? Well, each of the two Badrinath hikes were about five kilometers, so the elevation came quicker, and we peaked in less time. We started at 10,500 feet and passed 13,000 on each trek. Higher, but no AMS. It seems to be clear that my preparation was better, my weight was 7 or 8 kilos less and my fitness was sharper. My preparation for the motorcycle trip would be full and complete. I don't care if I was 73 years old. This was what my life was bringing me to. And the point of the spear was my Guru Deva, Anand-ji. I would not let him down and he, who had come to know me so well, would not have extended his hand with an invitation if he thought there was any concern.

12,500 feet in Badrinath, India. No altitude sickness!

I had reached out to several of my friends from Sattva to see if they got invites and were preparing to go. Graham from the UK, who was on the Badrinath trip got the go ahead and would be joining. Bill, from Durango, Colorado, a classmate in Sattva 300 hour and the Badrinath journey got an invite. These guys would be my rock.

The trip was to be fully staffed. We will have Royal Enfield, Himalaya model, motorcycles and a mechanic along for the trip. There will be Sattva staff as well as professional local crew who live in the mountains. Support jeeps to carry luggage and spare parts. All of the arrangements to visit the sacred temples and monasteries were handled. Best available accommodation in the Ladakh region and, of course, three organic vegetarian meals a day. I just have to show up, with a correct and ready heart, fully prepared, ready to open my wings and sail into this most remote region, most sacred of locations. I will be ready.

Today, I wired Badoni $1000 for the non-refundable deposit...yes, no going back for me.

Now is the time to load up an Amazon Wish List with: helmet, leather chaps and jacket, winter riding gloves, finally a good reason to get some sturdy and awesome Frye boots again, and big, military style duffle bags to use as luggage to carry all this stuff in (no worry about baggage limits in premium class flights).

Show Low Meets Lakshmi

Jump forward four months! I am writing in our brand-new mountain home in Show Low, AZ. It is a small city of 20,000 people, nestled in the White Mountains of Northeastern Arizona. We needed relief from the extended, blazing summer heat in Tucson. Last year, there were seven months of over 100 degrees F. You are forced into an AC life, venturing out with Koko, only on the early sunrise and post sunset hours of the day. Climate change is coming fast to the Sonoran Desert region. Why, even last month, the first hundred-degree day showed up two weeks earlier than ever on record in Tucson meteorological history. That alone proved our actions justified. Show Low is at 6300 feet elevation. 100-degree days are unknown. Maybe very low 90s, but cool, pleasant evenings, windows open all night. A short 180 mile, three hour drive from Tucson, it is a world away!

Koko is ecstatic. We are adjacent to the Fool Hollow Lake State Park, which boasts a rare (in Arizona) 22-acre freshwater lake. Before we closed on the final purchase of the house, we took her on a 20-minute walk over to the lake. She was in the water in a minute. Despite living the first five years of her life on Kauai, being in the ocean every single day and living on the river in Oregon for three years, this was her first time in the water since our holiday trip up to Seattle last summer. Very, very happy dog, as were her two-legged charges!

Last week, I walked out the front door and said to her, "Koko! Do you want to go swimming?" Her ears perked up and she began a steady pull on her leash directly to the lake, no directions or coaxing needed. The 38 degree water meant nothing to her. She is a retriever and there are geese and waterfowl out there!

Nonetheless, the mountain home already felt like our beloved place, and we tucked into all it had to offer. It is three bedrooms and at 1950 sq. ft it was half the size of our Tucson home. One bedroom became my office, yoga space and shrine location. Up went the Buddhist thanka with its centrally placed Buddha surrounded by 567 floating deities. Above that was the Sri Yantra painting. My shrine for this home was set up in a corner, graced by brass statues of Lakshmi, Hanuman and Shiva. On the floor was a 3' by 6' handmade Tibetan carpet that had come the Indian Ocean Trading Company, my original retail shoppe in Bellingham, Washington, in 1970. It was a perfect yoga mat. All in all, everything was continuing to unfold as designed in the cosmic consciousness. Kathleen and my days were filled with serenity and contentment.

I had been working with one of my students on a regular basis. The teachings were not of asana, but of a spiritual nature. I wanted her to learn the ishtas and part of that was through japa. We had been working for over a year and had swung through a number of deities. It surfaced in my meditation that it was time for Lakshmi! I normally shift my own japa practice to the mantras I pass on to her and we had just finished up Om Namo Guru Dev Namo. Yes, along with the major deities we can't forget the One within, the Divine Inner Guru. I next gave her (and myself) Om Shrim Lakshmiya Namaha. An honorific to Lakshmi, the goddess of wealth, prosperity, beauty and fortune. She is a consort of Vishnu (who himself had found a deeper place in my life) and part of the divine trinity, TriDevi, with Durga and Saraswati. Her images can be found in homes and businesses throughout India.

Japa and the accompanying mantras can manifest in very subtle and quiet ways. For me, japa practice is, in the most topical sense, is a way to set your mind in focus. To push the monkey mind asunder. And always, simply as a way to repeat the names of the gods over and over again, in reverence, bhakti and gratitude. And so it was that I had recited the Lakshmi mantra tens of thousands of times in the next six week period.

I need to digress here a bit in order to bring the story to fruition, so please bear with me a bit…

In November I sold my last Tucson rental property to a professor coming to the University of Arizona from the University of Wisconsin. He wasn't starting his employment until May, and he desired an extended purchase time before he took over ownership of the Waverly House. That worked out fine with me as January through May is the high season in Tucson and I could continue renting the home and collecting nice premium rents from travelers. Five months later my last tenant checked out on April 7th, about the time our contract called for a final statement of loan approval from the buyer's bank. The bank requested a letter from the university confirming that he had a job waiting for him.

Well, without getting too political in my discourse, I can tell you his request was turned down by the university. During this period, the US has a wannabe king running our country and he had put abject fear into colleges and universities across America. His directive was that if schools didn't hire the professors he wanted, sculpt their courses in a manner of his pleasing and teach with a political slant that professed his views on people and the world…that he would defund the federal grants that they all depend on. Universities weren't approving any new spending, promised employment or not. And my contract to sell the home, right there and then, fell though.

I needed that home sold and the mortgage paid off so I could in turn take the proceeds and make a payment that would make our new mountain home paid in full. What I ended up with was three mortgages: our Tucson winter home, Show Low summer home and the Waverly House rental, with no income other than social security. My outgo was double to triple my income. This was a bleak way to start my retirement! While I was steadfast in my fearlessness of all things financial, this situation did give me pause, as I wondered how the benevolent Universe was going to smooth the waters. Enter Lakshmi!

Two weeks ago, my old boss of 25 years, Diane, called me up and said there was big trouble brewing at the company and my help as a consultant was direly needed! Understand that neither Diane nor I had heard a peep from the company since our departure 5 years ago. Never once were we called for direction or information. And yet, this popped up, out of the blue. Lakshmi is always there and loves to pop up when you need her most! It is no secret in the business world that consultants earn 3-4 times what a fully employed wage would be. How dreamy...and then Lakshmi entered my consciousness. What else could it be, this highly unlikely event unfolding at the absolute perfect time? I have long since given up believing in coincidences. No, the past three years of my life have clearly defined coincidences and synchronicities as real, and I chalk them up as Cosmic Giggles. Divine laughter showing up in your life confirming that They are out there and holding me up at all times.

But wait! I still had an empty house up for sale! Well, one thing led to another, and I found a traveling doctor who needed a home for a three-month (ended up as a seven month rental) assignment. Pardon me, a traveling doctor found me (divine guidance). And just like that, all of my financial challenges had been met by answers just falling into my lap! Om Shrim Lakshmiya Namaha!

I have not had such a visceral manifestation of my spiritual work come to the forefront in the past. That is not to say I do not acknowledge the fullness of the grace in my life and how that grace has guided me for the last couple of years into and through all of the amazing experiences I have enjoyed with the revelations of the fullness of the Science of Yoga and the spiritual bliss that comes along with that.

ℒord, Let Your Plan For Me Unfold

June 30th, 2025

ℰxactly 2 months out from departure for Ma India. The anticipation is building. It is time to start accumulating appropriate supplies and apparel for the adventure. First stop was the Harley Davidson dealer in Tucson for a look at motorcycle boots, chaps and a leather jacket. I originally wanted to get some Frye boots, an old western brand of quality footwear. We actually sold them at my Michigan Indian Ocean Trading Company in the early 70s. Since I couldn't find a store stocking them in Tucson, I thought I would check out the Harley store. I guess I was continuing in the flow (with Lakshmi ever close), as they had a pair of boots that had the Frye look and they were 50% off...and they had my size! Perfect! I was off to a good start. Checking out their leathers, I was kind shocked at the pricing...way too high. I opted for Amazon and ordered some chaps, black leather with removable lining for cold weather riding. Next it was a gorgeous leather jacket, again with removeable lining for cold weather riding. It was going to be two and three miles up in the Himalayas, after all. I rounded out my purchases with a 25 liter tank bag that magnetically attached to the gas tank of the bike, some cold weather gloves and a kidney brace for those bumpy Indian roads.

As always, my mornings started with meditation, then a six round japa practice while walking Koko. My personal practice yoga sessions were going full steam. I was on the third go around of St. Karen's scores and scores of classes on SattvaConnect.com, the website which keeps us close to all things Sattva. I am on my second read of The Ramayana, the epic tale of the lives of Sri Rama and his wife Sita, who are

My favorite Hanuman statue, on the grounds of the Parmarth Niketan Ashram in Rishikesh, on the Ganga River

accompanied into the forest with Rama's brother, Lakshmana. On the journey, they meet many famous rishis and deities, the most famous of whom is Hanuman. Together they conquer the highest forces of evil in a fascinating novel of love, right-living and bhakti. During my spiritual work, the following prayer sprung out of my consciousness:

LORD, let your plan for me unfold in the exact way you have designed it, without any interference, hope or pleadings from me. Your plan is omniscient, and my dreams and false expectations are but a grain of sand in the ocean of your benevolence. Come what may, yin or yang, that your way unfolds in a manner that helps me grow, transcend and evolve. That is the manifestation of your love for me every second of every day.

DEEPER PREPARATION

July 30th, 2025

*E*xactly one month out from departure…Things are moving at a rapid pace now. The biggest news was the official notification from Sattva that the motorcycle pilgrimage will be filmed as a documentary, the final episode in the trilogy of Anand-ji's motorcycle pilgrimages deep into the Himalayas with his students. That was the whipped cream of joy heaped upon the bliss of the tour's anticipation. "The *Highest Pass*" was filmed in 2011 and *"The Road to Dharma"* was filmed in 2020 by documentary film maker Adam Schomer. These films changed my life and brought me into alignment and directly into the flow of where my life was destined to lead from the minute I was exposed to them.

Being a motorcycle rider for over 50 years, I was intrigued when I stumbled across *"The Road to Dharma"* in my quest to find the mysterious true world that existed behind the veil of western yoga. I had been practicing yoga for over 22 years in California and Hawaii, and I was desperately trying to find the actual spiritual gateway that yoga offered. The challenge was piercing that veil, as in most studios in the west, yoga had become a form of exercise, a workout and, yes, a space where you could be at one with yourself, your mat and your teacher. Here I was, exploring the Gaia television network, a place where the yogic, spiritual and metaphysical worlds were offered up. And here was a ten episode documentary about a young Indian teacher who took his students on a motorcycle tour on some of the most sacred spaces in the Himalayas.

He was not a bearded mystic of uncertain age, long grey hair and beard flowing, sitting in full lotus pose chanting. No, this was a handsome 36 year old modern man, someone I could relate to! I was drawn into the first episode. Transfixed on what I was seeing, I immediately devoured the next nine episodes. I had found it! Someone who could hold open the door of the beautiful spiritual world that I had been seeking for the last two plus decades. A teacher, a seer, someone who had seemingly found the answers to which I was yearning. He was charismatic, bright and cheery, and I was drawn to his message.

Following that introduction, I had a chance to get tickets to a Krisha Das concert in Los Angeles. I reached out to my son, a resident of that city, and said," Let's go!" He was all in. I was familiar with KD's work in singing kirtan as a backdrop to many of my favorite teacher's yoga classes. Long story short...at the show, the minute he started playing, tears poured from my eyes. I had no idea what was going on. I was not singing along or dancing like many in the old theatre, I was just crying. At that moment I knew that my life was changing, that the answers I had been seeking were going to come to fruition. That my life would never be the same. *A Calling* had entered my being.

Upon arrival home in Tucson, I saw that (Krishna Das) was appearing at the Telluride Yoga Festival the following month. He was having a concert and a class with Q and A. I signed up. The festival was incredible. After a nine hour drive from my home, through sacred Apache, Navaho and Ute Indian reservations, I pulled into the gorgeous beyond description mountain community of Telluride. I went to all KD's sessions (I actually had a chance to speak one on one with him for a few minutes) and his sold-out concert, filled with yogis who populated the town for the weekend. The changes in me were manifesting themselves at a growing pace.

I got home, researched to Sattva Yoga Academy in Rishikesh, India, where Anand-ji teaches and signed up for a three week 200 your yoga teacher training class. In October, 2022 I boarded my flight to New Delhi. That was my second trip to Ma India. Now, as I ready myself for the upcoming motorcycle trip, it will be my 7th visit to the Himalayas. No where else on earth feels more Divine, more welcoming and more like home.

The document requests started flowing in from the film production company. Lots of signatures and permissions. All of those involved on the film side were all Anand-ji students and Dharmic livers. They made it clear that they will be making sure that, first and foremost, they understand this is a spiritual journey for all of the people making the trip. They will be on the outside looking but from a perspective that offers all who wish to share their experience will have a chance to do so.

For me, since Adam's movies were the genesis of my new life, I was anxious to be a full participant. Anxious to share with the world what I was experiencing, witnessing and feeling inside. What I have found through Anand-ji's teaching has brought me to a life that is sublime, full of understanding and a complete and solid belief that the Divine resides within all of us. That the pathway inside oneself to the celestial world is filled with love, understanding and fearlessness. I want to bear my soul without reservation as a beacon of light for others to witness and experience.

The signature requirements were soon followed by a request to do some filming of myself on my cell phone so they could get some background information on me, my hopes and dreams, fears and anxieties for the pilgrimage. In the event I became one of the focus characters in the film, they wanted to be able to intersperse the back story. I was ready. Anything I can do to offer insight into the teachings I had been given by Anand-ji, my Guru Deva, would be seva (service) to the world.

The trip was going to require quite a few things to be purchased. I had not done cold weather bike riding since the

With my leather chaps, jacket (tag still attached!) and Harley Davidson boots that never made it to the Himalayas.

early 80's in Michigan and I needed to be fully outfitted for warmth and comfort. Joining the new motorcycle boots in my closet were a really nice and warm leather jacket and a pair of thermal lined, leather motorcycle chaps. I was important for me to honor the concerns my Fiancée, Kathleen, had about the trip. All the leather would protect me from scrapes and abrasions should there be any tip overs! I bought cold weather gloves (two pairs), long underwear and thick winter socks. A nylon tank bag that would sit on the fuel tank holding 25 liters of stuff. We would be well over 11,500 feet (3500 m) from September 5th to the 16th. Staying warm would be imperative.

While I had no altitude sickness in Badrinath, at last year's pilgrimage to Gangotri and the headwaters of the Holy Ganga River, my fortunes turned out a little differently. While this trek was rather similar in elevation rise and altitude, the walk was 11 miles (18km) and took all of the day. When we stopped for lunch, I was bushed and decided to take a nap. I didn't know it, but I clearly wasn't drinking enough water. I have been a runner for 45 years and "hydrating" was never a thing for me. When I awoke, Anand-ji sidled over and said that he rarely takes a nap, but I looked so peaceful, that he thought he would shut his own eyes for a bit.

Awake, but not necessarily feeling any fresher, we continued on until about 2 or 3 km from the finish, Pennie (a yogini RN) came over to me and asked how I was doing. Soon, Anand-ji was by my side, and they determined I had a pretty good dose of altitude sickness. (More about this in earlier chapters herein). I was bound, and most determined, to not have repeat of that! My research brought me to a medication called Diamox. I told my doctor about my trip and asked for a prescription which he was happy to provide. I think it should help, as on the motorcycle I will have no physical exertion like long distance trekking prior.

My physical and spiritual work continued. I was doing strong integrated classes with St. Karen every day on SattvaConnect. Meditation, japa, seva, Dharmic teaching. I finished up my second read of the Ramayana. At the Show Low home, I was doing a lot of hardscaping work with heavy pavers and sculpting my new property with mini drainage creeks to move the water from our Arizona monsoons away from my home's foundation into the natural flow down into the ravine where it naturally flows into a local lake. I have been sore every night! All for the greater good though!

During this period, I finally found some community seva. We live adjacent to the Fool Hollow Lake State Park. Every three days or so Kathy, Koko and I take a roundabout, three mile hike to the lake. The mission is the exercise from the walk, but primarily for Koko to go swimming. Once she sees the tennis ball in my hand and hears the word swimming, she is ready to go. She pulls on her leash the whole way. I throw the ball for 15 minutes and, as a dutiful golden retriever, she swims out with the Canadian geese, ducks and other waterfowl and fetches it, returning it to me for more and more.

We love this lake, there are so few in our Southwestern desert state, and one morning I stopped into the ranger station and inquired about volunteering. They were happy to have me and after a lengthy set of bureaucratic videos to watch and a background check, I was brought onto the team. As a result, I now have a whole new crew of friends and enjoy the joys of greeting people heading to our park for kayaking, Supping, fishing and camping.

Great people are working in the recreation field...animal lovers, nature lovers and all outdoorsmen / women. Fran is the Park Manager, and she does an incredible job of managing the park and staff. They gave me a couple of official polo shirts, T-shirts and a hat. I really wanted a shiny brass star with the word

Ranger on it, but that was not to be. Ranger T'Om has such a nice ring to it, at least in my head, but that will be another lifetime. I am a Volunteer. I can walk to work and I find it a great way to integrate into the community.

I am starting to dig in a little more. Soon I will be with my Teacher! I must be ready, be prepared, be able to loosen up and open my heart to all that comes. My meditation has a more meaningful footprint; the ideas and intentions are flowing forward. Today it was resonating with something that Anand-ji so often talks about…the Experiencer Experiencing the Experience. This life is completely mine. It is 100% what I make it. Why? Because when I leave this body, accepting the four-armed grasp of Shiva, to be thrust into my next life, this Life will no longer exist. Everything I see, feel and love will be gone. All that I have created will vanish into the ethers. This is why we talk so often about the Divine Within. It is from that Divine that the entire world, galaxies and universe spring…all created from the perceptions and sculpting that comes from within. And also, from without, as This is That and That is This. It not only manifests outwards to the infinite, but also inwards to the infinite. Exactly like there is always a beyond to the final outer edge of the universe, there is also a tinier within the smallest atoms. And somewhere in all of that infinitude lies the Atman, the Universal Soul. And in that Atman is where we find Unity, the ultimate goal of Yoga. The Unity that all of us share via that Atman, the point where we are at one with the All.

Anand-ji always reminds us that we are the Creator, not the created. That our destiny is held in our own hearts and hands. Leaning into the Atman we come to find comfort that The Plan for our lives is manifested from therein and when that Plan comes from Unity only Sat Chit Ananda is the result. Truth, Cosmic Consciousness and Bliss.

It is so clear to me that my entire life has unfolded in the perfect way for my life. Every single step of the way has been leading to the exact point that I am at now, keypunching away, filled with anticipation for three weeks with my Guru Deva, riding into the abode of the gods on the highest roads of the sacred Himalayas. So often I tell my students (and myself) Anand-ji's great but so simple saying, "Not why is this happening *to* me, but rather why is this happening *for* me?" From every step into the darkness, there is growth, transcendence and evolving into the light on the other side. For all the seemingly horrible things that happened in my life, each resulted in learning, knowledge and advancement after I passed through them. I was a better person on the other side. And each event, flowing one after another, day in and day out, led me to where I am right now. With a sense of acceptance, a sense of supreme and sublime gratitude for the Grace that has showered down on me, perpetually, throughout my life. That through all of it, here I am in the best place I have ever been, filled with joy, compassion for myself and all beings, diligently seeking a deeper understanding that allows me to, as sung by yogis the world over in the Gayatri mantra: have my heart be illuminated so I can shine forth like the Surya (sun) is shining.

So deeper I go, continuing with my japa mantra for Lakshmi, work which has already paid off with abundance and health. Round and round, over and over, Koko at my side, 648 mantras a day, well over two years now, keeping my thoughts with the Divine. Back home form our walk and rolling right into an online class with my beloved teacher, St. Karen. She keeps my mind and body focused and attuned. Never in my 25 years of yoga have I managed a yoga session every single day. I used to think I was so "Yogi-awesome" when I was doing three classes a week. But here I am at 73 years of age doing it on a daily basis, and looking forward to each and every one, as after each one, I am better, I am fuller, I am more content.

And loving each and every person, knowing they too have the Divine within, even when that Divine is not showing. This AM, post-japa, Koko and I were crossing at a corner on our return home. I had a guy honk, roll down his window and give me the traffic mudra (the finger) and rip off some swear words...all because he was going too fast and had too slow down a bit for the hippie grandpa and his pooch crossing the street. Oy Vey! Yes, hard to love, but you never know what is going on in his life, who or what he has lost, what has brought forth such early morning drama. Nonetheless, he too, is a human being living in the same swirl of life, with the same spark of Divine inside, perhaps covered up, but still there.

So, I work on my mind, body and spirit. Soon I will be kissing the ground at the Delhi airport, eternally grateful that Ma India has welcomed me home again. I will be ready, ready for what is to come, ready to accept all that there is before me. There will be challenges and there will be gifts, stumbles and sprints. Spiritual work is hard...you are not promised a rose garden of ease and smooth sailing along the way. Loss of attachment to the beliefs and things you have held dear your whole life can be rough. But one quickly learns that without the baggage of attachments, material or physical, the load gets so much lighter, your wings of love can spread wider and lift off is so much easier.

And, oh yes, 30 days and now out was the time when I would go into a full clear mind scenario. While my relationship with alcohol is very poor because of seeing it end a 43 year marriage...my ex-wife could not let it go and gave up her entire family for it. And my seeing oldest daughter suffer from the same alcohol addiction syndrome. I did enjoy the occasional beer or marguerita with my Mexican meal. Now, though, a cold stop. Also, time to stop my one drag a day marijuana scene. In the 60's, one big, fat, Bob Marley style spliff would get us as high as one puff of today's exotic blends. After 57 years doing it, it was easy to come and go, and this was a time to go. I wanted every part of me ready for the full immersion of the pilgrimage, my pure, unadulterated self.

Adair, a 51 inch Mexican Gopher snake living at Fool Hollow Ranger Station

The Infinite Universal Plan

It is the 21st day prior to my departure to India. It seems auspicious, even though I don't know why. Yes, 21 is a multiplier of the sacred three, the trinity…maybe that is it. Right off the bat, in meditation, I felt Anand-ji in the ethers. He was either thinking of his loved ones or sending out joy to the universe about our Wheels of Awakening Pilgrimage. Either way, his presence was real. As was that of my beloved mentor and master's class partner, Silvi, the German Warrior goddess who pushed me through the tough times of doubt and weakness during that training. Like I will carry the strength and openhearted love of Hanuman throughout the trip, Silvi's spirit will be riding on the saddle when things turn dark, tiring and challenging, pushing me on and up and out into the light.

So many things rose up I had to make some notes after so I could share my thoughts with you, dearest reader. As always, I am fighting back ego, either in terms of monkey mind or the more characteristic I, I, I. We had been asked by the documentary director to film a brief background story of ourselves, what the trip will mean to us, what our fears are, what we expect to gain. It is part of the process should they follow closely any particular person or persons throughout the journey.

I took this seriously! We were planning a trip from Show Low down to Tucson for the weekend, so I wanted to film on my yoga platform there which overlooks the three mountain ranges in Tucson, as well as the entire city. I wanted to do this at sunrise, after meditation, so I could be sure the words would flow from the right space. The directive said make sure your face is illuminated, so I sat in padmasana and faced east to film.

As always, Koko at my feet, my 15 inch OM brass plate with the Tibetan flags flying alongside. No reason to be nervous, as it would be the cosmic consciousness speaking through me. I just knew that I wanted to tell my story of how much the trip means to me. How grateful I was to Adam, the director and filmmaker, as his previous movies about the motorcycle pilgrimages of Anand-ji had brought me to where I was today in my life. Of my 55 year love of motorcycling, the mountains and most of all, spending time with my Teacher.

Yesterday, Adam wrote this back about the submission, "Thank you for sharing your video. Such a sweet soul you are." I was thrilled that they received my 3 gig video and that my intent had flowed through to him. However, this only intensified the ego mind…would I be featured? Today I realized that I wanted it not from an I, I I perspective but from a sharing perspective. Adam had, through his films, opened my eyes and my heart to Anand Mehrotra, the man who would singlehandedly push open the veil of yoga and bring me to my new and fuller life. My gratitude was immense. No, what I needed to do was share my experience, without fear or trepidation, for the world to see. How I was transformed into the joyous realm which I now inhabit. How my Guru had accelerated my transcendence, growth and evolvement. I wanted to share this great man with everyone, all those seekers like me, longing for a pathway to the spiritual universe. It was not about me. I was just the vessel and how my participation would unfold was not about my ego but about the Science of Yoga. A living testimonial of the Grace that had showered down on me since I first began my oneness with Ma India.

I was proud of the transformation in my life. All those family, friends and people coming into my life knew what had happened to me. Now, here was the chance for all of them to see, in the full spectacle of cinema, what my life in India was all about. They would meet my Teacher and witness what joy and bliss (the name Anand means bliss, BTW) he had brought into my life. They could view firsthand the glories of the sacred Himalayas, capture the spirit of the inhabitants of the highest villages, and witness my interactions with my Guru Deva. They would ride with me on the highest roads, feel the exhilaration of motorcycle travel in India through the chaos, serenity and majesty of the sacred Himalayas, abode of the gods.

Adam, through his film magic, would allow me to give the greatest gift of all to each one who sees the film. They would witness the rituals that are so foreign to Westerners, rituals that I was now comfortable participating in. They would hear the sacred prayers uttered by the rishis and, lamas, monks and pundits we would come across. Maybe they could even feel my anxiety, at first, of traveling on two wheels, on the British side of the road, as lories, scooters, cows and walkers passed by. The Gift! I was so proud to have a part in delivering it. My heart would be open for the Grace to pass through me to the film to the eyes of the beholders.

During this time, one Thursday I received a WhatsApp message from a long time friend with whom I had been teaching all the wonderful lessons I had learned in India. It said, "Please call me as soon as you have time". When I reached her later in the day, the following words came through the phone. "T'Om, today I went to the hospital and had a biopsy for a spot on my breast. The doctors are pretty sure that they see a small lump of cancer on the X-rays and MRI. I will get the results on Tuesday." She said that she had not told her husband or family as one of her children was having a long planned for wedding in Italy in four weeks and she did not want to rain down sadness or discouraging words on the celebration. I was the only one she told.

As you will read, this was a humbling time for me, as a teacher. What I would hear from her in the coming days would make clear to me that all the work we had done would come to bear in this situation. The way she approached this made me cry tears of gratitude. It was apparent to me that this dear student had taken the knowledge and put it to use in a time of her life when she needed it most. In fact, it clearly showed me that she had surpassed her teacher in understanding and implementing her hard work in the realm of the spirit. What greater gift could there be for a teacher?

She had risen above fear. She knew that out of this dark period that there would be light. She would show her children courage and steadfastness in dealing with adversity. She would use this challenge as a what is life *giving* me?, not What is life *doing to* me moment. She clearly understood that this had been placed on her plate by the universal plan, and gnashing of teeth, wailing in grief and tearing at her hair was not going to be the road which she traveled down. She would use her deep understanding of this life we are in to make this blackness something that would in itself turn to the light and create something from which she would grow and evolve.

This would also be the chance she had been waiting for...to show her husband and family that all the time and effort she had placed in learning about her new discoveries in the Science of Yoga had value and meaning in her life. And in their lives also as they would see her radiance and inner harmony radiated fully. They would see their wife / mom as the divine Warrior that she truly is.

Prior to this coming up, I had given her a new mantra for her japa practice. It was a Durga mantra. Durga is a Hindu goddess who is often depicted as a Warrior, riding a lion or a tiger, embodying strength, protection and motherhood. A perfect goddess with whom to ride out this challenge.

Earlier last month, I had asked her if there was any ishta that I could bring back to her from Indian and this upcoming pilgrimage. She quickly said that she would love it if I could find room in my luggage for a brass ishta of Lakshmi, goddess of prosperity and health. I am thinking the Infinite Universal Plan already was preparing her for what was ahead.

*L*AKSHMI:

*A*s I wrote in my book, *Living Fearless*, I am often completely enchanted and amazed by the power of the japa and the associated mantras. Sri Hanuman and his mantras carried me for almost two years. Through those times, when I needed strength, he was there. Whether it was on the yoga mat during a two hour Journey with Anand-Ji, or on a rocky trail in the Himalayas, his power could always be called upon to lift me up, to clear the monkey mind of doubt. I had a four inch ishta of Him that I would place on the upper corner of my yoga mat during every Journey. As one of the oldest student yogis I would often find myself directed to the first or second row in the big yoga studio on campus. Carried on by the Grace of Hanuman and the radiance of those on neighboring mats: French Ella, Hawaii Ella, German Silvi, Italian Bianca, American Courtney and so many others, I was able to rise up through the most challenging asana practices our Teacher would throw at us. How else would it be possible in a sea of 20 and 30 year olds? Not only the strength, but the bhakti love radiating from and for everyone, brought me higher and stronger.

As noted, I have been deep into Lakshmi in preparation for the pilgrimage. I have told you of the many instances of Her Grace and today, again, she reached a divine hand down and touched my life. I woke up receiving an offer for the purchase of my final real estate property. This sale will cement my retirement. It has been six months in coming and is received with bountiful gratitude. No more worrying about tenants, the home and all the financials, whether at home, on vacation or in Ma India. The culmination of a 33-year run as a landlord. And it will be finalized on the day before departure…bliss and proof of the

Divine and The Plan that has unfolded in my Life. Here, this 18 days prior to my departure for Ma India!

It was hard to stay focused in meditation, my joy was so overflowing. My Lakshmi japa walk with Koko was filled with light. Last night, I had made the decision to lean into Anand-Ji's Journeys on SattvaConnect, and that session followed japa. It was, at the time, his most recent video and I was prepared for anything he served up. What I received was over an hour of sublime and deep Kriya practice (not one asana!) which was focused on I am Atman Brahman. I am of the Soul of the Celestial. I am the creator. It was so reverent, so full and inspirational. As always with my Guru Deva, my tears flowed freely. As they flow now as I type these words, with Shantala's Baba Hanuman playing on my computer. My vessel is full of gratitude, overflowing. What Light has been brought into my life! What Grace! Since finding The World Behind the Veil of Western Yoga at Sattva, I am complete.

I don't want this to sound like a Christmas letter, filled with nothing but good news of the past year...I have been guilty of sending out many of those over the decades. I am clear in my world now that in this Lila life there is also darkness, struggle, challenge, despair. I no longer fear when the yang arrives. My growth needs it. I need to work through all the potholes in my path. Fifteen months ago, my youngest daughter, Pakayla, estranged me. She never told me why. Just completely ceased all communications. There is pain and sadness from this, but I worked with it daily and arrived at this point. She is a grown woman, 39 years of age. I raised her well and she has found great success in her chosen field of art. In effect, she has detached me. I have come to understand that sometimes love is like this. Each of us has given the most we can to each other, and as we grow and mature, sometimes our paths of life spin off in different directions. I am letting her go, with gratitude and deep affection in my heart. She has a solid foundation, she will prosper, I will prosper. I cannot carry the burden of sadness from missing her on my shoulders. I am freeing her. She will always be my daughter, and I imagine she will come back to me at some time in the future, but in the interim, my life must continue with growth and wonder.

No, it is not all wine and roses but to have found the Inner Divine is the greatest gift of life. I have received that gift and the flower petals that fall from heaven all around me will be that which I celebrate. A woman whom I love and am marrying, an over-riding sense of joy and contentment. How could one not wish to share this with the world...the close in world of family and friends as well as the big wide world of all those who inhabit this blue planet. This is my hope and prayer for the Wheels of Awakening pilgrimage and documentary. If I can touch one person, one life, as mine was touched, the Hanuman heart residing in me will swell with gratitude and thanks.

That Hanuman Heart

Oh my! One week out from departure. And Lila life's continuing saga moves along, too. As quickly as it happened, the house deal fell through. Lakshmi's grace turned south, and another route was apparently chosen for me. While it was perfect when it happened, I am secure on the belief that it is just as perfect that it didn't happen. I don't know what will come of it, but every inch of my life I celebrate…because it is MY LIFE, I am the creator and even if I don't know what is the Ultimate Plan, by God, I am going to celebrate every moment of the grace that showers down on me, come heaven or high water.

I have been working super hard in my Show Low yard putting in heavy paving stones, moving rocks for irrigation creeks and shoveling dirt. I get sore! I have literally moved 7 or 8 tons of rock / stone. So yesterday I decided instead of a yoga class, I was feeling the need to sit down and do a wisdom class from Anand-Ji on SattvaConnect. I tried to find one I hadn't heard before and picked on from February 23, 2025. It turns out that I watched this one live, but I was happy to review it again. Why? Because this was the talk where Anand-Ji answered a question I had sent in and he spent an inordinate amount of time talking (it seemed) directly to me. He referenced Gaumukh pilgrimage where he and Pennie walked with me during my altitude sickness. Also, the Badrinath trip, which was so powerful, where our group was snowed upon on two separate times, *when the sky was completely blue and cloudless*. He spoke about after the Badrinath trip how 8 of us on went on motorcycles for a ½ day trip up into the mountains past the Sattva campus and how all of the people riding that day had signed up for Wheels of Awakening.

I was beyond inspired! He was so excited even back then for the trip. Not only for his amusement and pleasure, but for the joy of traveling with all of us dedicated seekers and his beloved students. I cannot wait to get in my Guru Deva's presence again and continue to grow and evolve, to soak up his infinite knowledge and receive the blessings that come from being in his radiance. That is what this trip is about. Transcending to new levels. To make my sublime and content existence even more fulfilled and aligned.

The prior day, I had my final class with my student who had, in fact, found that she had breast cancer. She picked up my call on the WhatsApp feed we use for the class and there was this buoyant and glowing woman. So thrilled with her spiritual progress and how so much had gone right in her world since our class last week. No sorrow, no dread, no "Why me?". She had done deep and thorough research after her first oncology appointment post-diagnosis and joyfully related how she had found the absolutely perfect doctor to work with and perform the surgery. She laughed telling me that the woman had done her internship at the University of California San Francisco teaching hospital system, as it was the same world class cancer center where I had my own prostate cancer healed. Once her choice was made, she heard from many others that her chosen physician was absolutely The One, one of the best of the best in the southern California region.

She talked to me clearly (and ever-so-correctly) about how grateful she was for all the work we had done that had led her to the point where her entire outlook on this cancer diagnosis was one of fearlessness. Yes, there was fear, but it was flowing through her and not getting stuck, not being the core focus point. She was so thrilled that she understood that this was happening for her, not to her. That only good would arise from this, for both her and her family. She had been assured that her cancer was completely treatable in this modern medical universe, and she would be a beacon to her family, friends and all her came across her.

I was flabbergasted. More evidence that the work we had done together, of which I was purely a vessel of cosmic consciousness, was bringing its fullness and grace to light. As I have said, she has learned so fast, done so much work, practiced relentlessly. Now it was apparent to me that she had begun to surpass my Sattva Master teacher's level in spiritual growth and understanding. This surely rises up to be one of the great gifts in my lifetime. Her classes over the past 20 months have all been offered up to her pro bono and the divine manifestation of this seva on my heart was massive. Anand-Ji has helped me understand that the foundation of a fully expressed Yogic life is meditation, and always leading from the heart, that Hanuman heart.

DEPARTURE DAY AT LAST

Saturday, August 30th, 2025

Ok then, let us continue…

Departure from the house for Tucson Airport at 5:30 AM. What joy, expectation and delight. I am leaving with a firm foundation at home with Kathy being uber supportive of my experience. Koko will take care of Kathy and vice versa. We were back in the Tucson winter home where she feels most comfortable. She was relaxed.

As was I, surprisingly enough! The buildup had already built up. Now I knew I was in the hands of the Divine, that Divine that would lead me on this entire trip. While I would be the experiencer experiencing the experience, that experience would be as the Inner Self unfolded to me.

I stumbled out of the car with my two 49 pound suitcases, my 30 pound carry on (I had brought 24 of my first book with me for the store at Sattva), my small mini backpack /shoulder bag and my Sleep machine which I thought would be desirous in the high altitudes. I made it to the check in counter, thank the gods in Tucson that is only about 25 yards from the curb. My portable handheld scale proved accurate with my weigh in at home and the American Airlines matched numbers exactly. The bright orange preferred handling tags were attached to the baggage.

I zipped through the checkpoint and boarded my flight on schedule. About 15 minutes en route for our 90 minute flight the pilot came on the intercom and announced that at my HUB city, Dallas, Texas, the DFW airport was being shut down completely for weather and we would have to divert until the weather passed. No worries! I live fearless! Everything was laid out for me, and nothing could get in the way. During the shutdown, no planes would come or go so I would not miss my connection to New York nor the one on to Delhi, surely. I knew nothing is easy when traveling on these spiritual journeys and any bumps in the road would only make me stronger. We landed in Houston for the diversion. The pilot announced because of the issue on Dallas; many planes had been diverted to Houston and that there was not a gate available for us. We ended up sitting on the tarmac, waiting for a gate for 2 hours. The 90 minute flight had suddenly turned in four and a half hours. Finally at a gate, everyone went to the bathroom and got something to eat...I was fasting so just sat and read for an hour. They announced re-boarding. Away from the gate we pulled, only to be told traffic control in Dallas was a mess and we would have to wait on the tarmac...again, for two hours!

OK, now I am getting edgy. I did my deep breathing, said my prayers, appealed to the gods. And we entered the skies again for Dallas, got there uneventfully and landed at last...for what would be another two hours on the tarmac, waiting for a gate to open. If you are doing the math, that made it nine hours with the time to fly back to DFW. It took us an additional hour then to crawl to the gate...yes, ten hours in a 737, which had run out of water, food, had only one working toilet left. Everyone was grumpy, pilots, flight attendants and passengers. The trifecta of travel nightmares was unfolding right before me. The American (hereby referred to as AA) software was slow and overwhelmed, but I was able to garner that my flight to New York had left, without me and my luggage. It was also apparent that my New York to Delhi flight had left also during my tme on the tarmac.

In the end, and in retrospect, I realized that I probably should have spoken to the flight attendants, with whom I was well acquainted now, and asked to lead a seated yoga class. I know the whole plane would have loved it. Just too shy to pull it off, I guess.

Oh, to be challenged! Make me grow, let me transcend! Out of the dark comes the light. Because of my two million plus miles of lifetime flying with AA I had access to preferred phone lines. I called for help, the AI answering system told me I would get a call back in 90 minutes! Bring it on. I can take it! I searched out the airport help desk and, I kid you not, the lines were over 200 meters long. This had turned into the most discombobulated travel journey I had ever had in those 2,000,000 miles. I was determined to live fearlessly. The call back came and 45 minutes later I was rebooked to London, to Helsinki to Delhi. Sadly, the customer service agent goofed something up and my flight record went loco in the airline's system. Sitting on the plane to London, I waited for a one hour call back from customer service. She changed the Helsinki flight (which I would have missed) and booked me on British Air, Heathrow to Delhi. Perfect. The system was showing nothing about my luggage, But I would get there. Spoiled me was unhappy as I had to fly coach to London, where I never have been on international flights. I didn't care. Get me to Ma India. I was sardined in next to a MAGA air force vet from Oklahoma on one side and a Finlander, going to Helsinki and beyond on the other. Once the plane took off, I asked my Fin neighbor if she wanted to compare horror stories from the day of travel. I was sure I would win this test! Nope, she had left Tampa on Tuesday, four days ago, to go home and was delayed all that time. I put my proud tale of woe between my legs and accepted defeat. No matter how bad it is, stop whining, someone always has it worse!

The MAGA seatmate on the other side was a talker and I just chose not to be politically engaged, just listened, to all the stories...The COVID pandemic was fake, University of Oklahoma is now a WOKE university, The whole US military situation will be much better under King trump and all the senior admirals and generals that he fired were all DEI (diversity, equity and inclusion) hires anyways, from the Biden administration. And on and on and on... I popped half of a five milligram Ambien sleeping pill and went to sleep (as a contortionist). I was thinking about how all of my lean yogini friends would be just comfortable, but my 6 foot 98 kg bad self just didn't fit!

I know...how can this continue, T'Om? Well, I got off the plane and a remarkable woman in customer service in the British Air Club helped me get things sorted. Still no sign of my luggage though. My Delhi gate was a good 30 minute walk away, so I headed down there with plenty of time to spare. I got to the gate, went to the bathroom, fiddled with all my stuff to make sure I had everything, and what did I discover....no frickin' cell phone...surely, I must have left it on the charger in the BA Club. Thanking the gods for putting so much challenge before me and on my plate, I grabbed my 30 pound roll aboard and began the over a mile sprint back to the BA lounge. Oh yes, I was hot and sweaty when I arrived to discover the phone was not there. The same woman was at the desk...no one had turned it in. We called the phone and, praise all gods major and minor, someone answered the phone. They had just handed it over to the check-in desk at my Delhi gate, where it fell out of my pocket unbeknownst to me.

I was in serious jeopardy of missing the BA flight now, and dripping sweat, I rushed back the lengthy trek. They had just called my class when I pulled up! I walked on the plane, cell phone in hand now, to my premium economy seat, which was looking like a pillow in Nirvana. To make things better there was no one sitting next to me. Seven hours later, after 5 hours of blissful sleep, I walked off the plane in Delhi, kissed the ground and literally floated down the escalator past the majestic, giant hands displaying the various mudras, to the premium class immigration line, where, as always for me, there was no one in line. BOOM, straight to my favorite money changer who has a small table set up, mixed right in with the luggage carousels. I knew my luggage wouldn't be there. The AA service desk was only open at night, and this was 8:30 AM IST, September 1st, so out the international arrivals door I went. Predictably, there was the Sattva driver, my name on his clipboard and we charged out into the crazy Delhi morning traffic. Never so happy to see traffic chaos in my life.

Saving you the math this time, that was 37 hours of unbridled chaos and struggle, departure to arrival. Oh, I was being challenged, but I was up for it! Fearless! I could surmount anything put before me. Bring it on!

Arriving at Sattva with a Strong Back

September 1st, 2025

Six hours later we pulled down into the Sattva driveway. 43.5 hours after leaving my home, I kissed the ground at Sattva, my home in Ma India. And checked in, sans luggage, and with no info about my bags from the airline. I was issued a room on the third floor of building next to the boutique. 42 steps up to my room. I was glad I didn't have my two 49 pound bags! Like in the Gangotri pilgrimage last year, I was adjacent to Anand-ji's radiance, his penthouse home just above me. Ommmm.

Alice and Uma got me checked into the Wheels of Awakening group in the office area, handed out the swag: hoodie, T-shirt, wooden bead mala. I was able to take a nap prior to the 5PM Welcome Circle. Ahhh.

The welcome circle was in Shakti Hall. I was so surprised at how many people would be accompanying us. They announced 52 riders and passengers, 6 Sattva staff, and unknow number of motorcycle support (mechanics, etc). Then there were four people from the documentary filmmaking production crew…Adam, the director and producer, two camera guys, Scotty and Rama and sound man. We would be a Shiva force in his abode!

Anand-ji told us that we have come from all over the world, arriving here together as a family, as a collective soul. He spoke to us about thinking on the Grace that has all of us here at this minute. The infinite possibilities that had to come together in all our lives to have us here, together, at this moment, from literally every part of the globe. Unity, I kept thinking...this is yoga. He spoke about his father, who had stumbled on Laxman Jhula with no intent whatsoever of living there, and ended up staying forever. At a time when Rishikesh, and particularly Laxman, were basically country outposts, the ancient home of the rishis. He said in his youth that elephants would come into their small village en route to The Ganga for water. Now it was a city, monkeys maybe, but no elephants.

I looked around. There were old friends: Bill from Colorado and his wife, Beth, Graham came in from London, Pennie, our enlightened nurse. Friends from previous classes and pilgrimages.

We went around the big circle, and everyone was given chance to say a few words. I said, "I am Atman Brahma, my name is T'Om. I have come here to be with my Guru Deva, to further evolve in his teachings and to open my heart to the experience of being in the abode of the gods in the Himalayas. My life right now was all about living the Gayatri Mantra, witnessing the radiance and light in all. And expressing that love and light in every footstep of my life."

I had in front of me a tiger eye stone carved into a heart, given to me by my beloved fiancée, Kathleen, as her support and love for my pilgrimage. I had also carried to India with me a sacred bald eagle feather, retrieved from an ancient Apache Indian settlement where a small group of people lived by a creek centuries ago. The area had petroglyphs, arrowheads and broken ceramic pieces. It was a secret area, and I was getting a tour from the Park Manager at Fool Hollow Lake State Park, Fran Sorensen. Her love of nature filled me with awe and respect. In her honor I will place the feather on the highest mountain we come to half way around the world. (I thought!)

Anand-ji then began the mantra that starts most events at Sattva:

Om Tare   Tu Tare   Ture   So Ha

for 108 rounds. I had done this many times with him and at my Master's training, whacked by jet lag, I closed my eyes, chanted and went far away. Next thing I knew everyone had left the room and my Guru Deva tapped me on the shoulder and we walked to the Havana together. I was determined to stay present for this round! Which I did but was still one of the last ones to gather flowers from the mandala design on the floor and bring them to the Havana ceremony, which for the first time ever, was held *inside*, in the huge Brahmananda Yoga Hall. Three havanas were lit and everyone gave up their toxic nature and created space for new prana shakti and kindheartedness. Then we all walked to the river and threw the flowers into the flowing waters, aarti-style.

I wandered into the office seeking Ramesh's help in calling the AA baggage service. The DEL AA gentleman was very helpful, at least after we got him to tell us that I would not have to drive the 12 hour round trip to Delhi to pick up the luggage when it came in. He said he had located the bags in Dallas, and he would push them forward and, when they arrived, send them up to Rishikesh. "Is it OK if you get them no later than the 15th?"

I explained the nature of our trip, made it sound like I was part of the film crew, and he quickly agreed to try to have them to me by the 4th. That would be perfect!

Dinner was served up shortly thereafter and we all continued to bond into One. I slept in a bed (not an airliner seat) for the first time in three nights.

Tuesday, September 2nd, 2025

With the help of an Ambien to beat the jet lag, I slept until 5:30AM...unheard of for the first night, twelve time zones from home. I was ready for the early morning puja ceremony, now at the newly constructed shrine on campus. During my master's training I had developed a true affinity for the early morning religious practice and would be attending each one of them at the 6:30 hour. From there, through the end of monsoon season light rain (for now!), I moved to the Sangha Café, below Shakti Hall, where I enjoyed my start of the day meditation. It felt good there because I was adjacent to my old friend, the Giant Buddha sitting by the river. With his low hanging ears, he had heard many of my prayers, entreaties and blessings.

Throughout these early morning practices, I was focused on the correct thought and attitude about my missing luggage. What does life bring **for me**, not what is life trying to do **to me**. It was easy to stay in the right zone because my focus began sharpening during my travel delays trials. I KNEW that everything would unfold exactly how it was meant to. And if it was meant to happen for me to have correct thinking about the situation, I was ready for the work.

It turned out this morning that "The Push" got my bags onto a flight to London, where they arrived while I was sleeping. However, there was no word today whether they had actually moved from London. I could only thank all the gods that they appeared to be moving...Lakshmi, of course, Sri Vishnu, Sri Hanuman! I had only my roll aboard with me, which was primarily filled with 24 of my books that I was bringing for offering at the boutique. Anand-ji had read my book when he was on an airliner for his 2024 US tour and told me I could offer it for sale on the campus. That left me room for two shirts, two pants, one pair of socks and two pairs of underwear. So, I continued wearing the same clothes I had sweated through during my travel to India.

I was time for our first Journey. Everyone was bubbling over with excitement. This is Anand-ji in his fullest expression, teaching, rolling us through a 90 minute practice. What would he bring forth? As I have mentioned earlier, he was trending away from asana-based Journeys into a full-throated, Kriya focused offerings. I expected this would continue…and it did. Not one asana. Nothing but Kriya! Of course, we had person to person eye-gazing, and it was beautiful.

Everyone left exhausted and filled with the correct knowledge that we were all exactly where we should be, doing exactly what we should be doing.

I cannot help but relate to you, and all experienced Sattvans will understand that this class was a first. It was the first time in six visits to the Sattva Academy that there were more men in the Shakti Yoga Hall than women. I didn't count, but maybe 30 men and 20 women. As a note, my 300 hour class was 54 women and six men, so this was a big switch. Tatia noted later at breakfast that she really liked the unique "Bro Energy" in the room. Bill said he noticed it when doing the OMs at puja, that the sound was definitely more bass than the normal angelic high tones from the assembled yoginis.

And another first at the café for breakfast! Baked Goods! I am serious! Can you believe cinnamon rolls, chocolate cake bread and another light cake bread. We all laughed and commented we hoped this was the start of a new breakfast pattern! It turned out that it was just a welcome surprise and not a new kitchen protocol. Sad face...

I took a moment to bring my books down to the boutique. I had brought 24 of my first books (dead weight in my rollaboard) and gave them to the shopkeeper. I told him that Anand-ji had said we would sell T'Om's book in the store when it came out. I donated all the books and told him that if by chance they sold out, maybe Jemina could help me get a publisher in India and we could offer them on a consistent basis. Amazon (my book is self-published) doesn't offer printing in India like they do in most other countries.

The talk we were waiting for, travel logistics, was at noon. We assembled to receive the fruits of all the work the office team had done to put together such an undertaking. Annemarie laid it all out, starting with, "This is India, you all need to stay aligned and in the flow. You all well know that in India, especially during monsoon season, things can and will change." The first change was we would be meeting at 5AM on Friday so we could all enjoy the six hour drive down to Delhi to catch our flights to Leh from there, not Dehradun, which is only 90 minutes away.

She then went over the details of the trip day by day, which will unfold as you read through these pages. The planning was an immense undertaking, and I honored their work righteously.

She invited Adam Shormer to talk, the head of the production company doing the filming and the director of the first two documentaries. He is a most likeable guy, very funny, and like all of us, an adherent of Anand-ji's wisdom. He said they would be filming everything, all the time, but our personal pilgrimage was the most important thing going on and at any time we felt like they were in our face or intruding in on a special moment that we should wave them off and they will cordially melt away.

That led to nap time, and I fell dead to the world. I set my alarm to wake me 50 minutes later and immediately found myself in the grip of a serious wave of jet lag. It just comes on like a tsunami, and one truly has to push hard against it to keep from lying down again and going back to sleep... submitting to the habit energy of your home time zones, as Anand-ji might say. I was certainly going to rally; it was to be the first Wisdom Talk of the trip and I wanted to be ready and alert to receive. Tomas' wife, Regina, had told me that Anand-ji's mastery is so complete that we can take nothing for granted, that there is a whole world of knowledge in every sentence. I never want to miss a sentence.

He started out with, "Don't resist duality! There is always going to be the yin and the yang, the good and the evil. Working through it is how we grow and evolve."

The remainder of the talk was on the three states of being: animal, hero and deva. The animal is living in the fear that the ego generates. Always protecting us with its false sense of safety. Keeping us in a box, holding us back from exploration and growth.

The hero is your consciousness saying I must change, I must become interested in my own evolution. Push out of the box. Grow. Changing the world begins with changing yourself. The world becomes real based on the experience of your own consciousness! The hero always must leave the known into the unknown, leave the familiar, rather than living in the perpetual doubt of the animal nature.

He told us that, "We are here at this moment because we are in our hero's journey, our vida is coming forth, making us a rare group who have chosen to be hero. We have found our tribe! With hero and vida life you are always home. You get a glimpse of God consciousness and the accompanying alignment. We find a natural ability to be with the Isness of Isness. You find that the hero's journey makes it OK to not be perfect, to be OK just being yourself. That you are choosing not to suffer!"

The third state of being is deva. In Sanskrit, deva means luminous. It simply means acknowledging that when you slip, it is OK, just get and carry on.

One of the subsequent questions for Anand-ji was, "Congratulations on becoming a father, you look great! I was wondering how your outlook has changed and if you believe your teaching will change as a result of your fatherhood?"

And Anand-ji he paused. I had seen / felt this before. The tears spilled from his eyes and he said, "Only Mahajan and Shreenaya (his baby) make me cry." I have on a number of occasions witnessed this when he was asked about Mahaji, his teacher. And here it was again with his baby girl. It was heartfelt. He said that when he first held her, all he could think was that he was holding humanity in his hands. That every child comes into the world in the same way, without any attachments. My tears flowed with his.

Later, after the wisdom talk, I spoke to Anand-ji for a few minutes. I told him he looks luminous and radiant as always. I needed to tell him about the power of Lakshmi in my life now that she was the focus of my japa. He smiled knowingly and I told him I think I had been an istha chauvinist, always giving my focus to the male deities…Hanuman, Shiva, Ganesha, Vishnu! He laughed at that one

Shortly thereafter we had some musicians perform for us…a sitar and table player, at the Sangha cafe. They were so good, so impressive, I truly would put them at Carnegie Hall caliber. As they were playing, Nena and the baby came down and stood outside the open door. Anand-ji was already swaying and thoroughly enjoying the show, and Neena handed the baby over to him. She was as radiant and beautiful as the mother of a newborn could be. Her husband wrapped his daughter in his arms and together they swayed away for quite a while. The trio brought joy to the eyes of all assembled.

The flower mandala on the floor for our welcome circle

Wednesday, September 3rd, 2025

Puja and meditation led me to our second journey of the trip and, true to my many observations, there was no asana, only Kriya. He led us through some serious and deep breathing work. We did about 40 minutes of breathing, along with breath holds and then it was, "OK, stand up and shake!" You have all been there and done that. The shakti was alive and well after all that breathing.

He then asked that we gather in groups of five for some deep and serious eye gazing, laying on hands and focusing on compassion. I can't fail to mention that our five person circle at the end of the Journey included Pennie, Ben, Dave, Cory and myself. Again, first time ever in that kind of circle with more men than women. I was in between Dave and Cory, both there for their first Journeys. Each of them had shoulder muscles twitching and undulating, and I could feel the Shakti bubbling up in both of them. I knew that both were having a transformative experience and it brought me great ananda to be with them and see it happening. After the Journey, Cory, whose fiancé, Elena I know well, came up to me, looked me in the eyes and his tears just started flowing. I knew he had entered the Sattva family. I was crying right along with him.

Cory was in our five-person circle

Off to breakfast where an announcement was made about an "easy hike". I had to pass as I was getting whacked with another jet lag wave. It was time for an early nap. Later, upon waking, I heard that the hike was to the Durga temple up the road from the Academy. I had been there a number of times, so missing it only affected me by not enjoying Anand-ji's talk on Durga. Given my recent interest in the Devi goddess, I would have surely enjoyed that talk, too.

I was during my 300 hour training that I asked Anand-ji if I could take his golden retriever for a hike up to the Durga temple. I was missing my Koko badly and this would be comforting for me. He said sure, but you must take the huskie, too. I was all in on that, but with the huskie I knew that I needed others to hike with me as the huskie was strong and a serious puller! I put the word out and had about ten others join in with me.

At the temple, the huskie, with Houdini prowess, somehow managed to jump out of his harness and charge into the forest after a stray dog. I stood there in shock, along with all my yogi friends. We hollered and whistled for a while, but he was gone. We all went up to the temple, and were all fervently working through every Durga mantra we knew. To no one's surprise, the huskie came trotting out of the woods and submitted to his harness. Every single person was thinking, what if T'Om had to come back to Sattva and report that he had lost Anand-ji's dog?

Surprisingly, though, during the day's Wisdom Talk, he continued about Durga, so I got some good instructive learning anyways. Maybe you can, too…

He spoke that Durga is there when you wake up and knows who you are. She is a fortress that cannot be defeated. She hides in plain sight. You awaken the Durga in you when you don't need protection. You don't need to call for her…she is within.

He then moved on to Dharma. And he started with, "Whoever is living in Dharma will always survive!" And the following phrases of his might be helpful to you...

Dharma-To evolve, gain Unity, expand our consciousness.

You are not here to prove anything, you can only learn! The ability to fulfill the need of the hour.

Belief is only helpful if it leads to knowledge.

Adapt your state to whatever it requires.

We do best when we mingle, not when we segregate.

He kind of went on then about guarding your mind from inappropriate penetration. He insists that we have to post doorkeepers to our perception, meaning you have to be alert and attentive to whose voices we listen, and what information we let be absorbed by our mind. Then, he ended with a classic Anand-ji line, "Sleep is a time machine that takes you to the future." It kind of goes hand in hand with his, "Intuition is remembering the future!" Because the Wisdom Talk started at 7:30 PM, when it ended, I was off to bed.

My luggage did not come this evening. I was going to chill until the morning and push myself to accept what this situation was that was happening to me. No matter what unfolded, I was ready to accept it, address it and rise above it.

With a Surprise Departure,

It Begins

Thursday, September 4th, 2025

I woke up to the news that the luggage had not made it to Sattva and was still in Delhi at the airport. Ok, breathe, do your puja, get in your meditation.

What was the plan that was going to come down from the cosmic consciousness? Listen and know that I am the Creator. I needed to go to Delhi. The bags would not make it to Rishikesh in time for the group departure tomorrow morning. I would miss the Journey this morning. As it turned out, Anand-ji was a no show and someone else hosted a yoga class, so OK. I hated missing the fraternity of the 3AM ride to Delhi, but our numerous calls to the baggage company made the decision quite clear.

The office called a car for me; I went to my room and put together what little stuff I had and waited for the driver's arrival. The car pulled up and it was Rajeesh, my driver of many Rishikesh / Delhi excursions. We had a great time laughing and talking for the whole six hours. He was also in touch with the baggage guys and, as it turned out, they pulled into the Andaz, my favorite Delhi airport hotel, just as we did. I was so glad, the early departure effort was worth it, and I would have all my gear AT LAST! My determination and work had proved worthy...until they only took one suitcase out of their van. "Sorry sir, only one bag. We still cannot locate the other!"

OK, more challenges, more learning, more of life unfolding. Ma was bringing me a sense of detachment! The bag that did come, was filled with my Sattva clothing...shorts, tank tops, t-shirts. I was grateful for a full array of bottoms and long sleeve, heavy tops that were in the bag. But no motorcycle gear, no underwear, no socks, long johns, leather jacket and chaps, my heavy Harley Davidson boots, tank bag, gloves. Meh! I was going to Leh tomorrow and it absolutely all would work out.

I bid Rajeesh farewell and walked into the Andaz. It felt like home in Delhi. A few of the staff remembered me from past stays (white yogi with long grey hair and all, not their usual client) and I checked in. The Andaz is always only 8000 Hyatt points and for the quality that they bring it is one of the great bargains in the Hyatt collection of worldwide hotels.

My great friend from Tucson, Oscar Campos, had joined me in becoming a points professional. When I met him, he was a yoga teacher at my local studio, running great energetic and bright classes. I am pretty certain, as the owner of the Nissan dealer in Tucson, that he is the only car dealer in America that is also a Class A yoga teacher. I turned him on to the universe of airline and hotel points, and having a PhD in math from Dartmouth, he picked it up quickly and turned it into a science. A car dealer can easily put 100s of thousands of dollars on cards each month. In no time he was flying the world over in first class, staying in suites in the most beautiful hotels in the world. He accumulated so many perks that some spilled over to me. Like suite upgrades, one of which I used at the Andaz that night!

More than double the size of my normal room, it had a super big bathtub and after wearing the same clothes for 5 days, it was time to soak it all away in the hot water immersion. The bath did me in and I was in bed at 8:30, hoping this would be the night that I would get in a solid eight hours. It was not to be...up at 3:30AM, still jet lagged.

Leaving Andaz

SEPTEMBER 5TH, 2025

What was the plan that was going to come down from the cosmic consciousness? Listen and know that I am the Creator.

I repacked my suitcase and carry-on, went online and prepaid for my excess weight baggage with Indigo Air ($35), our airline to Leh. Watched CNN a bit, wrote, passed the time until The Breakfast. I did not visit the waffle pancake station, nor the full bake shop with its delectable delights. I spaced the big Asian food area and the big Indian food area. Yes, I managed to be an insufferable pig with everything else, from omelets to lassi, tropical fruit to cheeses, but come on, I had no clue what kind of culinary adventure was in store for us in Leh Ladakh later today.

No word from the AA baggage people so I went ahead and checked out and climbed into my Andaz airport car for the quick zip over to Terminal Three. Ok, it was looking smooth and easy, much less traffic than at the late night / early morning hours, when so many of the international flights depart. The police checked my boarding pass and passport before I could enter the departure halls, easy, peasy. Walked up to the Indigo counter and got in line. I promised myself not to take for granted the blessing that I had in traveling in business class so much of my life, as the line toiled, snaked and moved slowly forward. Made it to the counter things were going quite smooth and then the agent popped up with, "That will be $35 for the excess weight fee, sir." I mean heck, what can you do? I had already paid last night. She said I could go over to the call center office and hash it out with them. That was certainly not worth $35. I would just request a charge back on my credit card when I got back to America. The good news was she didn't charge me for excess weight on my carryon.

Rare short lines at the security check point and I threw my bags up on the conveyor. Greeted the officer at the end of the track with an Om Namah Shivaya and he uttered the same back at me. Then, he asked me to open my roll aboard. The contents flew out, and he proceeded to go through pretty much everything, sending my laptop, my sleep machine and a few other things back through the Xray. All good. In the Flow. I stuffed everything back in and realized my jacket was gone. A Sikh officer looked around and found it. I was searching my brain for the religious greeting for him, and it wasn't coming. As he approached it popped into my brain, "Wahe Guru". He smiled and repeated it back to me.

Out to the gate to wait for my tribe, we boarded without incident, and in flight, everyone just stared out the windows at the majestic Himalayas passing under us.

Normal chaos at a foreign land's arrivals gate greeted us. I was filling out the foreigner arrival sheet and the pen I picked off the table popped from the elevation and royal blue ink shot everywhere...my hands, the table, the floor. Lord, I accept all these challenges. Bring them on. I have a serenity about all of it now. Whatever comes, comes. All part of the flow.

There was a whole team from the support group to meet us. They grabbed our bags, and we were off through the streets of Leh to our hotel. That is when I noticed that it was clearly a Buddhist majority town, perhaps even one formerly of Tibet. There was a big sign over the road of His Holiness the 14th Dalai Lama, whom I honor each morning while facing north in meditation. The red, yellow, blue, white and green (fire, sun, water, air and earth) Tibetan prayer flags were hanging everywhere. We pulled into the absolutely gorgeous Rewa Hotel, which would be our Leh home.

It has to be noted now that the Badrinath host hotel was a three-star affair, the Gangrotri a one star. In Leh, the Rewa is a full on four star, with a beautiful lobby, Tibetan woven art on the walls, much wooden wall and ceiling coverings. IT HAD AN ELEVATOR! Everyone was simply ecstatic. I was given my room, 201, which, here, as it most parts of the world, is on the third level. I opened the door and stared in disbelief. I was so shocked that I started filming. Ravi, who was doing the Sattva video and still photo work for the trip was next door, said, "Here let me film you!" King bed, couches, tables workspace, a heater, a TV (which would go unwatched), large picture windows overlooking the mountains. Sublime black granite walls in the bathroom, which even had amenities. Waterfall shower as well as a handheld. A screen that rolled up so you could enjoy the mountain view while showering. This would be our base hotel for much of the stay. I was flabbergasted with ananda! And I hadn't even enjoyed the bliss from the kitchen downstairs yet.

Lunch followed and the buffet was filled with all the exotic foods you would expect from the area, overflowing in its abundance. They even had my favorite, apricot juice, which doubles as a helper to overcome altitude sickness. All of us were buzzing. The bonding of our tribe was changing into second gear.

After lunch, a nap...so welcome...but up in time for the Wisdom Talk at five, went downstairs and found it was moved to six. No problem. We are all learning to be in the flow. No being anal! Nothing is fixed. Whatever comes and is to be, comes on its own schedule. I went back to my room and spent some time writing, chronicling.

I should mention that it was now clear that the film crew was always ever-present. They would not miss a moment of the outside and most likely, at indoor activities catch quite a bit of what was going on in the inner selves. My hope was for them to catch as much of the inner side of things, particularly the Inner Divine of the tribe. I would try to get as much down "on paper" for the book as I could, figuring even with three cameras and eight to ten episodes, there would still be much that ended up on the editor's floor.

In addition to my heart pill regimen, I have now added Diamox, a prescription medication used to help push off the effects of mountain sickness. I started two a day on Wednesday night and feel they are helping. Ladakh sits at 11,500 feet in elevation, and I am doing OK up here in the clear blue sky mountains. Additional help in that regard also comes from living in Show Low, where the elevation is 2000 meters (6400 feet). That, too, is a big help. Anand-ji said last night the next practice would be a "non-sweaty" one. Chill time, let the body settle in...

Our wisdom talk was sublime, as always. Here are some highlights:

Don't only focus on what is happening on the outside, these mountains and their glory. Pay attention to who is making this scene for you. The majesty of the Himalayas, His playground, it all points to the Inside. If you allow it, they will take away all the unnecessary, leave room for growth

It is a rare privilege that our group, our tribe, is all looking for the same thing

Each individual has to have total responsibility for the group space. Be together. Be mindful to talk with appropriate intention. Have aware conversations.

Don't be the same person leaving as the one who arrived!

It is not what is being seen, but what is the seer seeing where the experience is happening.

The vortex is much more accessible here than in so many places...especially Las Vegas (That got a big laugh!). Get into the state where the scene is happening. Be aware.

The seer is a vast field, waiting to shift.

There is no such thing as the thing...just the dance.

"I stop seeing the traffic. I just see the way."

The awareness of the seer is so still, so soft. Hear the energy. Open to the possibility where only love happens. Find a baseline state of love in your life.

CHOOSE YOUR MOTORCYCLE AND LET'S GO!

Sunday, September 6th, 2025

I am telling the story of this day just as it ends, because today ended up being one of the greatest Dharmic days of my entire spiritual life. I need to "get it on paper" while I am feeling it, because I don't know how long this feeling will last (I hope forever).

The day began with a welcome note, I woke up at 6AM, having gotten up just once to pee...remember, we are overhydrating! Maybe, just maybe, on day seven of my travels, I have beaten the 12 hour time zone change jet jag. The airplane nightmare screwed it up at the start, normally it only takes me five days, going eastbound to India, to beat it. So, I can only hope it is defeated...but enough on that as I don't want to jinx it! The passing nights will tell.

I enjoyed some time talking with Kathy at home via WhatsApp and writing in the book and then headed down for a breath practice. Ramesh met me right away and said not to worry, we will get everything you need, and sure enough, a bit later, there appeared with a monster tech riding jacket with protection plates, zippered pockets and adjustments galore. Also, some knee and shin guards. All of my needs were being met, despite no luggage.

After our usual sumptuous breakfast (nothing like the Andaz though!) we went outside to choose our bikes. I really wanted one of the black bikes with metallic gold wheel rims and

Royal Enfield Himalayan Bat Bike

Jen, my first passenger, friend of Courtney from my 300 and masters

highlights. It was my Batman Bike. Jen was my first rider, and she had a bit of an issue getting a helmet, right to the last minute...with 40 bikes leaving, many were needing attention. Consequently, we were one of the last three bikes to leave the parking lot. The others had disappeared! We would have gone the wrong way if there wasn't a traffic cop standing auspiciously at the end of the drive who was able to direct us to follow the others.

First stop, though, petrol. It was quite a scene at the station with 40 bikes all crowding in for service. My Bat Bike took 12 litres for a total of 1050 rupees to fill it up. We left the station en masse, quite a site for the locals, I am sure, and in less than 10 minutes we were at the Angala bridge and left the city behind. The roads were unbelievably smooth and perfect for motorcycles. I was determined to stay in the front group and work my way up. I did just that, until I was directly behind Anand-ji, our point of the spear for this journey, basking in the tailwind of his full radiance. Jenn and I stayed there most of the day. We enjoyed some GREAT riders in our group, but maybe not any who had been riding for 55 years like me, save Peter. Today, I would live my fearless life and bring it all to bear. My Warrior biking attitude paid off and kept us out front, riding on the left side of the road and all. We wove in and out feeling the smiles and joy of all the riders. Everyone was in the flow.

We stopped at the beginning of the 5 km road up to Matoh Monastery outside of Ladakh. It was our first stop, and everyone was exhilarated. I was particularly thrilled because I was in the flow with my two wheels, in the mountains. Everything was perfect. My rider, Jen, was exhibiting great passenger skills and it was as if I had no rider at all. In the Flow! The Royal Enfield pulled powerfully and flawlessly. I was at one with the motorcycle. I wanted to spend the first day in the tailwind of Anand-ji's radiance and I did so, right on his tail for 75% of the ride. We have great riders with us, and I was simply not going to slouch it!

After a 20 minute break at the gateway to Matoh Monastery, we were off. At first, a long slow climb, and then we reached base of the mountain on top of which was the monastery. As always, there were the twisty, turneys with deep fall aways that represent so much of Himlalyan riding. It was steep, but it was also short, and we squirted out onto the parking lot, greeted by a ten foot tall, eight foot round prayer wheel. As everyone pulled in, Anand-ji told us a little history of the place and told us to go ahead and explore, find someplace to meditate or contemplate. From the upper reaches I could hear the monks chanting, music from Nirvana. I knew right where I was going…straight to the temple. So up, up, up the steps I went, passing the giant courtyard. Incense was perfuming the air.

Then up to the temple, shoes off and into the sacred space. Into another world, a world of detachment, a world of love, a world of spiritual bliss that oozes out of every crack. The chanting was going on full. About 16 monks. I bowed to the big Buddha in the back of the room and moved to a seat on the outer wall. I sat back on my heels, vidrasana style, and enjoyed the thick, four layers of Tibetan rugs cushioning my legs. I looked around the holy place. Ornate carvings, all colored in fantastic detail and vibrancy. Brass Buddhist statues of all kinds. I was surprised there were no thangkas, but it didn't take away for an instant from what I was experiencing. I listen to music of Tibetan monks chanting regularly, but to be here, hearing it live, taking it all in in the manner intended, brought me to my spiritual knees. I dropped in. I began my japa practice and did six full rounds, my head and body weaving to the hypnotic music. When my japa was over, I dropped in deeper. I started to lift off into the cosmos. The music touched me as deep as any sounds I had ever heard. Tears were flowing, I looked into the eyes of the monks and wondered what their lives were like. All the work that they do, not for themselves, but for me and you. A radiant sense of Love was flowing in the room.

I could have stayed all day, but their chanting came to a close. I am sure that they would have given their all for each and every one of us in that room.

They filed out of the temple, and I followed right behind them. Across the large courtyard into other buildings, maybe to lunch, I don't know. Adam also trailed after them. As they dispersed, I turned around and walked back through the gate entering the vast courtyard. Just past the gate, I simply broke down. I was heaving and shuddering with tears cascading down my cheeks. I had my chi greatly moved up on that mountain. Sam was there and as she had witnessed my floundering and came over to hug me. It felt good. Person to person, a big Arizona hug.

Sam, a meaningful hug at the perfect time. Arizona people stick together.

I wondered down back to the motorcycles and saw two younger monks coming down the road from the temple. I walked up to talk to them, to tell them how much their lives meant to me, that they had given up their every material possession to live a life of service to their community and the world. I told them I was ready to join and asked if they could cut my long hair right this minute, short and monkish. They both laughed and said, sure, follow us.

These monks at Matoh Monastery were happy to cut my hair and have me join them!

We have all had sublime religious experiences which open doors and permanently change us. This was one of those times for me. I truly felt at that moment I could have joined them. I laugh now, thinking about my privileged and sheltered life. Could I really do what they have done? Given it all up.? All of it?

Down the mountain we sailed, I felt like I was flying. Garuda to be sure. We went home the long way, motoring along, mountains to the left, mountains to the right. We crossed over the river and headed back towards Leh proper. Smooth, smooth riding, riders passing, riders falling back. Quite a bit more traffic on this side of the river! We pulled onto the Angala bridge and just like that we were in the city. It was busy. We had a couple of near misses and *just worked to find a way through, not seeing the traffic.* Surprisingly, I had the closest call of my motorcycling career this day. We were a km or so away from the hotel motoring down the street and a car door opened, fully, right in our path just five meters ahead of us. I swerved away and missed that door by only a centimeter or so. Later a fellow rider told me he was riding behind me and was shocked we didn't hit the car and go down. We are protected! We had become separated in the traffic and I didn't really have a clue where to go when the Jen yelled, "There's the gas station!" Perfect, we went past it, did a U turn, flowed through to the next traffic circle (all on the left side of the road, mind you) and spun off onto our street. We parked the bike and Jen and I hugged. A day never to be forgotten

I feel I need to mention at this point that the time and effort I put into this book had a cost. As I was tucked in my room working away, I came to understand that I was missing much fellowship and personal interaction with the bulk of the tribe. It was a clear cost, I understood, but it was important to me that I get everything down in the evening or no later than the next day, because things were coming so fast and furious and I needed to document it all. And with my 73 year old brain, that meant putting it to paper as soon as possible…otherwise the possibility of events leaking away was real.

I say this now because Jen and I had a mutual friend, Courtney, who had taken a Sattva training class with Jen and another couple with me. Courtney is a radiant and charismatic yogini and when she told me I NEEDED to meet up with Jen, I took it to the bank. On the last day of the pilgrimage, I gave Jen my first book and she gave me her new book, *"Atlas for Lost Souls"* just off the presses. She surprised me by reading mine in a day or two while I was traveling home. Her compliments on it, coming from the professional writer she is, melted my heart.

I started her book shortly upon returning home. It was engaging! It was beautifully written, and she drew me into her world of extraordinary travel experience and the phenomenal outlook on travel that is the basis of her book. I thought I had been a voyager! Not even close!

This made me realize that in my author's absence, hunching over my keyboard, hunt and pecking each word, that the price of my documentation was greater than I realized. I could have spent days talking with Jen. And yes, acknowledging each and every person in the Tribe had an incredible story behind them that brought them to this pilgrimage. And I missed out on so much of this. No regrets as this is how things unfolded and after all…I am the creator. It was my making, so that is my life.

Back at our luxury, in my mind at least, hotel, I showered and prepared for a Wisdom Talk. Day Two was as sublime as it gets. Perfect in every way. Just what the Divine had planned for all of us. We were growing as a tribe, as a two wheeled sangha. Our Guru Deva was leading the way.

Notes from our Wisdom Talk:

Our intention is to grow, but this is life, so you never know.

When you get initiated by fire, no one wakes up excited to jump into the fire. You never know when the time comes. It is almost a complete surprise, but it does come at the right time.

The sync of yin and yang is constant

When you are in it, holding it in your sacred heart Is It!

Can you come to the point where everything that happens to you comes to Love?

Life is not about you being right.

Kali shows up the minute you least expect it. (Like the fire...she is the fire)

Nothing is under control, yet everything is under control.

Our bodies have downloaded the knowledge we need for this trip. Where do I go when my expected actually happens?

Oh yes, I noticed at the Rewa, that once again, my room was directly across from Anand-ji. I wonder if it happens by accident, or if he feels like I need his sheltering wing. Either way, I accept the path of the cosmic consciousness wholeheartedly!

Our First Two-Wheeled Long Distance Ride

Sunday, September 7th, 2025

Up for meditation and down for breakfast. I sat with Adam, the director, and he shared with me some drone footage that they had taken at Matoh Monastery. It was stunning. It gives the full breadth of the scenery from the sky view and films from where the bikes cannot go. He, too, was very excited about it. I asked him how many episodes he was planning and without hesitation, said, "Ten, I want to show it all!" That was thrilling news for me as the broader and more complete the filming of the journey and the stories, the more OUR deep feelings and life changing experiences would get out to the world. The depth of Anand-ji's message and wisdom would more fully percolate into the minds and hearts of those watching. This was my reason for joining, so that as many as possible can find a door opening, know where to look to as a start when they have received a calling from their hearts to find the secrets within. A bonus for all of us would be for our extended families and friends to get a true look at what we have all been doing, having our lives changed by this Hinduism. Not too scary after all!

We had a short logistics meeting after breakfast and prepared to depart the hotel for Alchi, where we would stay the following night. My Mountain Sickness was completely under control. Whether it was the Diamox or the lack of long hikes, not sure, but given that Alchi was about the same altitude as Leh, I stopped taking the Diamox for a few days, at least until we were preparing to have some serious higher elevation changes in the next few days.

For today, my passenger would be Leanne Brueckner, a long time Sattvan from Australia. She had never been on a motorcycle for this type of riding, and I wanted to make her feel as comfortable, safe and secure as possible. We were going to travel in three groups of about 12 bikes for this stretch and the rest of the trip. I had gotten my Warrior biker spirit out fully yesterday, riding with the Hanuman wind, and felt I could leave the front of the pack behind for a while, chill, mellow out and more fully enjoy the scenery. Ravi, a teacher and main photographer from Sattva, would be our lead rider. He is an accomplished motorcyclist and set a great pace.

My two day passenger, the illuminated Leanne, on the right. Mauritian Sophie on the left, Taylor in the middle.

After about 25 km we came to a collective stop. We had passed klicks and klicks of military bases, as large as I have ever seen. The Indian government was serious about their historic threats from Pakistan and of course, China, with whom they shared a 2100 mile border. There were constant skirmishes with both countries and northern India is filled willed military support for garrisons on the far northern outposts of the country. Someone suggested that the broad smooth roads we were enjoying were built primarily for the military. They are truly fantastic road builders, easily equal to the European ones and their mountain traverses.

We re-entered some serious mountain driving, twisty roads and sheer drop offs. We rode another 25 or so km and ended up at the confluence of a couple of ancient rivers, the Indus and Zanskar, easily a kilometer across. There was rafting and zip lining. Being a Sunday, the were many motorcycle clubs out. At our stop there were well over 100 bikes, a couple of different bike clubs and 100s of people. Almost all the bikes were Royal Enfield, just like ours, the (now) proud brand India bought from the British decades ago, and greatly perfected. One guy had a shiny new 1300GS BMW. We spent a lot of time talking to him. He was the club leader of 50 of the bikes there. He was a rider! He had 30,000 km on his new bike in the first year.

I bought a package of the small almonds that are popular in these parts. I purchased them from a local lady with only one tooth in her mouth, but she had a full smile. The small bag was, I thought, 60 rupees, but I only got 110 rupees back from my 200. I was happy to let her keep the extra.

We departed and wound our way for the last 30 km, down to the charming village of Alchi, our home for the night. After a full lunch, we were standing in the lobby waiting to check in. There were about six people there, including my Guru Deva. You know, I always take every chance I can to kid and tease him, because he is often teasing me, along with his other tease target, Jemina. Knowing he was in earshot, I stepped up to the counter and said, checking in," I am Anand Mehrotra". Now that got him going and I could hear his hearty laugh over my shoulder. I told him I thought that was the best way for me to secure the finest room! More laughing.

The market near our hotel in Alchi

In the room I went and discovered a beautiful hotel room in a sublime location, but it was shades of Gangotri, as there was no heater. No worries. I opened all the windows and let the beautiful mountain air in. I suspect the temperature was 60 degrees F. Next on the agenda was a nap. Turned out to be an error, as my nighttime sleep was interrupted and I really can't say I got my third 8 hours in a row.

Post nap, I noticed that there was a little bazaar area hidden a bit behind the hotel. I did a walk through, as is my norm, to get a lay of the land, size up the vendors, getting a feel for the haggling scene and what happens after the "first best price, sir". I let some gifts reach out and say, "I am special and you need to take me home." I will come back later in my time here and lock down some purchases. Turns out that I didn't make it back, except to buy some homemade woolen gloves, as we only stayed one night in Alchi and I thought there were going to be two.

It was an exciting night as a fire ceremony was on the agenda at 6:30. We came downstairs and saw a big ring of plastic chairs had been set up around a large oval havana and it was filled with wood. Anand-ji started with some breathing and grounding advice. After a discussion of letting the Saraswati Devi influence into your life, the ceremony then moved to 108 rounds of a Saraswati mantra, The mantra was OM, then silently to yourself AIM (Bija word for the goddess), Saraswatiye Namaha.

Again, Anand-ji brought us all together into the flow. The mantra rounds passed quickly as the fire burned, and our hearts opened up. At the end of the mantra, on a windless night, there was a gentle puff of breeze, which lasted only 15 seconds or so. Hanuman made his presence felt with that quick and soft breeze, blessing our tribe along with the goddess Saraswati.

Anand-ji then asked us all to conjure up the greatest, most important thing in your life that you wanted to throw into the fire and remove from your consciousness. Then mentally remove the toxic and make room for the blessed shakti. He said he wanted to have us think not of our own intention to burn the bad in our lives, but to think of all around the circle and be supportive of everyone's success in doing the same thing.

He directed five people to his right to stand and walk to the fire. Stand before it a minute and pray for the removal of that which needs to go. Then kneel and grab some rice from the bowls below and toss the rice and your most desired thing that you wish to remove from your life into the fire. It ended with all of us holding hands around the fire. Soft words from our Guru Deva, and off to dinner.

I had an enchanting dinner conversation with Sophie! I thought she was French but had no idea that she was many generations deep from the Island of Mauritius. I had to confess I had no idea where that was, I thought it was in the Med, actually. When she told me it was in the Indian Ocean, south of the Seychelles, I perked up. Very few Americans had been to the Seychelles, but I had managed it on one of my round the world trips. Her island is off of Madagascar, was very close in nature to Kauai, where I had lived for over a decade, and when I looked it up. Mauritius. I saw it was 20 degrees south latitude and Kauai is 22 degrees north latitude. I felt like I could relate to her historical stories of being a trading stopover for many nations and a melting pot of many cultures. An oasis in the sea.

I, being so damn shy, am trying to make my way around all the dining tables at all the various stops. You might say, "Sure, T'Om, you might be shy, but once we engage you, we can't shut you up." I am working on that! I am just overflowing with Bhakti Love and it gushes out when the spigot is tapped. My life has been so blessed and full since finding Anand (I understand now that this has always been so).

That life, from which I have no regrets, that has for every minute of my life pointed me to exactly where I am at this minute...deep in the bowels of the Himalayas, with my great Teacher. I want to shout it from the mountain tops. I want this dogma to be available to everyone. And it is! No one is excluded, no matter your race, sex, color or beliefs. There is room for you. You can make Love your baseline for everyday living.

LAMAYURU, LADAKH, INDIA

Monday, September 8th, 2025.

We were up early as Anand-ji wanted us to head down to the ancient temple in Alchi. We trailed down, past the small market, where all the vendors I had talked to yesterday were happy to greet me as I was walking by, again promising "new best price today." I had figured out a few things to buy and told them all I would be back. The group made it down to the monastery, which is said to have started construction around 1000AD and finished up about 1050 AD. It is on the high banks, above one of India's most famous rivers, the Indus.

Walking into the first of the four temples, the timelessness of the place was immediately evident. The paintings on the wall were ancient; the Buddha statues clearly came from another time and place. Walking on the wooden floors, thinking about the centuries of monks and townspeople who had trod on the same hand-hewn beams, sanded smooth by bare feet and feet in stockings. I found an appropriate spot and meditated for a while.

I moved on to the second temple and was doing the same, when a villager walked in, he wore local clothing and began chanting. I fell into a trance. His chants and mantras were coming out of his mouth so fast it was making my head spin, imagining the years of worship that filled him with such grace and majesty. He went on for about 10 minutes, with everyone in the room in spiritual awe. Then he stopped, stood up and said, in localized English, "Thank you for being here in our Alchi temple. I am a local villager and come here every day and pray and chant in this manner. I do not come here to pray for me and my earthly circumstances, but for the world and all sentient beings. Our religion wants to send out our prayers to heal and make the world a better place for all who inhabit it. This same kind of chanting has been going on here for over 1000 years."

I was taken aback. Here again, the light of Tibetan Buddhism shines bright, for me and you and all eight billion of us, no matter their individual circumstances. These monks, villagers and lamas daily sending their Love our way.

I walked down to the overlook view of the river on monastery grounds. Three or four hundred feet down a steep cliff was the film crew, filming a woman meditating right on the river. How I love these guys. Their professionalism, determination and desire to get as many stories and as much footage as they can from the group, with the Himalayan backdrops that are so sacred and mighty. I sure wasn't going to the river; I would have needed a vernuncular to get back up! But there was the film crew, getting another story. I continued to be so thrilled from hearing they were doing ten, one hour episodes. Such a journey, so much unfolding every day, such scenery, so many stories.

We all meandered back to the hotel for departure preparation after a wisdom talk in the restaurant area at the hotel. I stopped to make one purchase, some hand knit wool gloves. Both my pair of biking gloves were nestled securely in my lost luggage. There was the potential for colder riding today and tomorrow, so they would be needed.

We all gathered for the Wisdom Talk before departing on our motorcycles. When that was over, we loaded our belongings into the luggage truck and other vehicles that accompanied us. I was supposed to have Rhonda for a passenger today, but we got our signals crossed on dates and soon the joyous passenger, Leanne, was up in the seat, riding for the trip to Lamayuru. Group Two took off, although Ravi our group leader was nowhere to be seen...off quickly, I guess.

It was quite a ride. The villages were getting further and further apart, and we were going deeper and deeper into the mountains. The scenery continued to be seemingly from another world. Traveling along the river, always, with steep, drop off gorges down 100s of meters, and the high mountains up. We wound our way for about 65 kilometers and were starting to see our first signs of some serious road deterioration. There were rock falls that had just been pushed aside by the heavy machinery of BRO...Border Region Organization...the world's best mountain area roadbuilders. In some spaces the fallen boulders and rock covered a whole lane. On the riverside of the road, boulders on the highway had fallen off and down the precipice into the gorge. Those areas were marked by outlining the fall off area with rocks. You did not want to feel the road give way on that side, to be certain. As always, the roads were twisty, incredibly curvy, but being on a bike made the challenge fun. Hopefully for my passengers, too.

We stopped for gas as a group in Khulti, always bonus for station owners, but probably maddening for locals, that is if any Indians ever get mad behind the wheel, which I have never seen, anywhere in India. No matter the situation, no stink eye, no traffic mudra (the finger), no shouting...just drivers finding the way. Our bikes full, off we roared the final stretch to Lamayuru. In no time, we pulled into the Grand Moonscape Hotel. They were ready for us with French Fries! tea and other snacks. My top floor room had a balcony and a view of the entire valley, the monastery standing majestically over it all in the distance

My great friend and Ladakh neighbor, Graham.

I went out on that balcony and there was Josh and Graham on either side of me, we being some of the ones who had booked single occupancy accommodations for the trip.

I enjoyed a long Dharmic discussion with Josh Stone and it was a bonding experience for me. When I first arrived at Sattva for the trip, there was Sherifa from my 300 hour, whom I sadly did not recognize at first glance. And she was traveling with Josh. That let me know early on that he was a Dharmic brother, as Sherifa is firmly seated on the path, teaching the Sattva method in her homeland of Kuwait as a Master teacher now.

Late that afternoon, the rain started to lightly fall. Our cars took us over to the monastery where they had arranged for us to sit in for a session with the monks chanting. Like the Alchi temple, this one was also 11th century, and it had an antique feeling to be sure. The ancient paintings on the wall, the crumbling building, but still alive and serving the community. We were told to go to one of the lower temples and about 15 of us wandered in and meditated in the holy space where this had been done for over a thousand years. After about 20 minutes, we were retrieved and directed to gather in the main temple. Like the Matoh temple on our first day on Leh, it was resplendent and vibrant with color, religious art, brass statues. The rows of elevated platforms running perpendicular to the Big Buddha, were covered in Tibetan rugs for the comfort of the monks. As a focal point and backdrop over all stood a 15 foot high, 1000 armed Buddha, peacefully overlooking the temple's inner sanctuary. We didn't know what to expect, but we got the full Monty!

After sitting there, my eyes popping out of my head with the Buddhist art splendor before us, the monks started walking in. First, they made sure we were all comfortable, then they sat down and those who played instruments had them delivered them by the rookie monk. I was so thrilled that even though photography, not to mention a four man Hollywood film crew, was strictly prohibited in the inner sanctum, a deal had been struck (even monks want Big Screen PR for their monastery)! To know that what was about to happen would be completely filmed with three cameras and a pro soundman made me ecstatic.

And they began. First it was all chanting. After their warmup, they took a break and a ten year old monk brought around a big tray of cups and handed them out. Then, in came the two liter bottle of Coke and Sprite (O America, the things you have given to the world). A thirteen year old monk entered and helped with the welcoming drinks. Everyone's thirst quenched, the chanting started again. And then the drum, the horns and the bell, rung by the head monk sitting on elevated cushions so he was above the others. It was a lovely ceremony. Throughout it all I kept thinking that the clarion call of the bell really had true meaning for me and it punctuated many of the chants. The steady rhythm of the drum was hypnotic. (A few days later Anand-ji would refer to the bell and its importance to everything in the ceremony. Same with the drum, but the bell is king.)

After 45 minutes it rolled to a finish. Once again, I cannot get enough of it, these monks chanting. I did not have the celestial experience I had at Matoh Monastery, but the sound bath definitely opens doors every time for me. I was thrilled it had been fully filmed!

The film crew for the Wheels of Awakening Documentary in Lamayuru

Lamayuru Temple and mountain backdrop

Back to Leh

Tuesday, September 9th, 2025

We rose in the normal fashion, all of us getting in our morning meditation, had breakfast, mounted our trusty steeds and began the drive back to Leh. I had as my passenger that the sweet sounding Dharmic vocalist, Rhonda. I swear we had a great time. For some reason I could hear her voice better than the other ladies (wind direction, speed, not sure) and we talked and babbled the whole way. I asked her to break out her mystic voice and give me a voice massage. I encouraged it, wanted it, needed it. What followed was such a lovely concert of earthy sounds from times gone by and times yet to be. I am guessing she was an American Indian in a past life as much of it resonated from that group. It was healing.

Most of the road was backtracking where we had been before, the roads were wide and smooth, as seems to be most true in the lower altitudes, if you can call 11,000 feet a lower altitude! It was a 120 kilometer day, but as I said, smooth and fast riding.

We made it back to the Rewa Hotel just after noon. It was always a joys to return to The Rewa. It was our home in Leh, there were no surprises, only a comfortable room, great food and a hotel full of Our Tribe.

All my passengers: Jen, Leanne and now Rhonda, had been real cosmic gifts to my adventure and I hereby express my sincere gratitude to each of them for their trust in me and what they brought to the pilgrimage in Royal Enfield saddle.

We all got re-checked in and had the afternoon off. I took the time to head back to the Army Navy surplus store just down from the hotel. For two cents on the dollar I bought some long

Rhonda, always aligned, always in the Flow

underwear, a woven military green belt (will work great with my State Park Volunteer outfit), three pairs of socks, one of which was a pair of flannel lined, thick, fleece socks which would surely keep your feet warm in the Arctic Circle. I'm pretty sure all of that was under $6. We had a sumptuous dinner at the Rewa and I retreated to my room to write. Did I mention that there is a proper chair and a desk in the room? I wrote until 10PM and called Kathleen. It was a good sleep before the Big Day.

Sitting on Khardung La, 18,379 Feet

Wednesday, September 10th, 2025

Today, my lost suitcase, with all the motorcycle gear, found its way to my front door in Tucson!

It started out as a normal day, 11,000 feet up in Leh, in the Ladakh region. It ended up being the best day of my life.

I woke up at the lovely Rewa and leaned over to check my messages before meditation. And there it was, a photo from Kathleen, of my missing piece of luggage, at my front door in Tucson! As I have talked about, I put a lot of Dharmic energy into knowing that all my travel woes, from missed flights to lost luggage were just one of those challenges put before me. That it is what it is and I am the creator of what happens in my life. That I truly had no control over what was going on (I know, despite being the creator!) and somehow the end result of it all would end up benefiting my life. That photo was such a blessing. Such a gift. It was not lost but found. And I wouldn't have to wrangle with the airlines for replacement. Nor would I have to schlep that 22kg bag home with me! Big bonus!

Most of all, as I looked at the situation, the thing that stood out most was that I didn't need the bag, even though it had all my motorcycle gear and cold weather clothes. Here I have been in India for 11 days and I have survived without it and its contents just fine. The Sattva staff found a bike jacket for me and through the 4 or 500 kilometers in the Himalayas I had ridden, I have had all my needs met and been more than comfortable. The Universe delivered for me in what was my perceived time of need.

I went downstairs and shared the news with my tribe...I was the only one of 52 that had a lost bag. All rejoiced. We had a hearty breakfast, and the announcement was made that we should get gas in the hour before we left. Dern! I was going to do that last night but after I bought my stuff from the army / navy surplus store on the street, it started raining. So, this morning I jumped on my bike and road to the gas station, less than a klick from the hotel, filled up and reckoned with the traffic circle...left side driving...and was back. I dropped my one big suitcase off at the hotel lobby for storage during the 3 nights we would be gone, threw my roll aboard onto the luggage truck. I went over and bungeed by backpack to the bike seat (thank you Greg Cyr for the bungee loaner and delicious lemon protein bar). All 12 of my Trader Joes bars were in that suitcase now at my house!

We gathered outside the hotel on the big lanai and formed a circle and Anand-ji did a group blessing and we were off. We were going to Khardung La and traverse the highest motorable road in the world, at an altitude of 5602 meters, or 18,379 feet. That was an 8000 foot rise only 39 meters from Leh.

Today I had decided that I would travel solo, no passenger, as I had no idea what to expect in terms of mountain altitude sickness and felt it would be imprudent to put someone else at risk. The rise was swift and the views unparalled. We stopped at 15,300 feet for a short rest and bathroom break. This was higher than Washinton's Mt. Rainier at 14,410 feet and California's Mt Whitney at 14,494 feet, the highest mountains in the lower 48 states of the US. A Lot Higher. I was riding slower, more in the middle of the pack. Lots of gravel, potholes and sheer drop offs mixed in with the great roadways. At this point, I was grateful for my new long underwear and heavy socks, I had two pairs of pants over those, and two shirts under my heavy jacket. For the first time I pulled my balaclava over my head. It was getting cold and we still had 3000 feet up to go.

My Royal Enfield Himalayan 450 was performing flawlessly. After four days of riding, I experienced the sensation of being at one with bike. I knew its capabilities, and it knew mine. It was road cycling at its finest. And just like that, we were at the summit. It took me a few minutes to notice that I was completely unaffected by the altitude. Completely! I chalk that up to three things:

1.) The fantastic logistical preparation by the Sattva staff that had us at around 3500 meters (11,500 feet) for four days, acclimatizing.
2.) The Diamox prescription Altitude Sickness meds I was taking.
3.) The fact that there was no strenuous mountain hiking, just easy motorcycle riding.

We all celebrated. This was The Highest Pass. This assault was one of the primary reasons we were all on this pilgrimage. Photos were taken, snowballs were thrown, snow angels were made. For me, it seemed like a true success story. All the preparation over the last eight months. Overcoming the Mountain Sickness that I had on the Gangotri trip. And I suppose also, being the grandfather of the group, actually doing it at all! Sam took a picture of Anand-ji and I that I will forever treasure.

The summit was getting crowded. This was peak summertime high season, as well as the time when most of the road work was done before the winter weather made things very difficult to accomplish. There were giant pieces of road work equipment competing with us on the roads. It was time to leave. We headed off and stopped after about 25 meters as the huge dump trucks and earth moving equipment made their way in the opposite direction. As always in India, the chaos on the roads somehow resolves itself and we started moving over the pass for the long downhill journey. Feeling full of myself for not being sick, I was ready again to ride with the front group. I poured on the power. Soon I was number four or five. The lineup would change, and people would move forward or be passed and dropped back. It felt invigorating to ride with some of our great riders rocketing through the Himalayas. My bike and I were in alignment.

Anand-ji led me to greater heights than Khardung La, for which I will be ever grateful. He is my Guru Deva, my Teacher, my Master.

With the help of Diamox, and spiritual righteousness...no Altitude Sickness

Greg, Torsten, Anand-ji and Jenn, who was in the last documentary, back for more, all festive on Khardung La pass

Torsten ripped past me with his orange, white and black riding suit. He was always in the front-of-the-pack of the riders.

One of the photographers had a most impressive driver who could have easily had an great pro motorcycle career. He would frequently whiz by me, passing on corners and long sweepers. The photographer later told me he trusted this guy with his life, and it was a surefooted investment.

We all pulled around a big left curve, and I saw a bike on the ground, and rear view mirror out in the street. It was Torsten. He had caught the lip of the road, and his front wheel just couldn't negotiate the four inches back up to the primary surface. Gods being with us, he was OK, standing up in no time. All the bikes stopped.

I hung for bit and then decided to continue to ride down the mountain to let the 6 or 7 bikes, including Anand-ji, that were ahead of Torsten and had no idea what happened, know the situation. After about five kilometers, there was Anand-ji, riding back up the mountain. We met and I told him what had happened. He continued back up the mountain to check on Torsten. He would never let anyone go unattended. Ever!

We regrouped down the mountain a bit and drove another 20 minutes or so to a chaiwallah that sat adjacent to a beautiful mountain stream, clear as the Himalayan skies. Young cows were lounging there and as I sat down, one came up to try to get a lick a of my chai or any other goodie I might have about me. It was warm, after the 18,000 foot 35 degrees F.

Jen and Josh by the chaiwallah stream

We lounged for a while, the camera crew got lots of filming and we were off again, next stop about 45 minutes later at the km101 Dhaba, a rather large restaurant with outdoor seating, under canvas, for about 80. We had a big, well-prepared lunch, and another leisurely rest. I feel like the temperature must have been approaching 70F...at 12,000 feet! We were grateful for the shade.

Then, a most unusual thing happened. It felt the 1.5 inch tiger eye stone, carved out like a heart, in my pocket. Kathleen had given it to me so I could hold her love while I was gone. And ten minutes later when I felt for it, it was gone. Vanished! The guys at my table all searched around on the floor and it was simply poof! Gone. It troubled me as I had lost one that she had given me one my Gangotri pilgrimage. I blamed it on the Altitude Sickness! I was thinking of excuses I could conjure up as we rode off.

About 45 minutes of riding time in and I was back to being in Anand-ji's tailwind. We pulled off onto a road leading up to a temple. We could see the giant Buddha, overlooking the vast valley, resplendent in vibrant colors, typical of the temples. We got to the top of the long road and were stopped for admission. Well, it turned out the governor of Ladakh was in town and he was worshipping there. Our Teacher thought it would be better if we came back tomorrow so we could sit in a calmer and more peaceful environment. I concurred. Back down the mountain we went.

Our hotel was about 10 minutes away. We pulled in with the normal varoom racket when we arrived anywhere. It was a little bit of a chaotic scene...one of the rare times on this trip, to the credit of the Sattva staff and their travel agency! We were splitting into three hotels. After some confusion, I got next to Ramesh and saw that I was not staying at the main hotel but was at the Organic Village Resort. We left our bikes at the main hotel and cars took us over to the Organic, less than a click away. While I was a bit verklempt at not being at the main hotel, ours turned out glorious! Everything always works out and for darn good reasons, way above my pay grade with the gods. So nice in fact that all the group talks and practices were held at the Organic! We had HEATERS in our rooms, which were yurts, by the way. And scalding hot water! I settled in easily and quickly.

In our quirky world on the road, it turned out that the same governor who was at the Big Buddha temple, was staying at the main hotel. That meant bodyguards and guns around. The Organic was the spot! All of us over here were enjoying the serene vibe of the hotel, waiting for Anand-ji to show for a wisdom talk. When he arrived, he was immediately challenged to a game of badminton, which he readily accepted. We all knew he would be all in, and he was!

They set up for the wisdom talk in our large courtyard and we gathered around. He said after the events of the day, he really didn't have much to talk about and took questions. When done, everyone went back to their own hotel for dinner. I finished up at about 8PM and went to my yurt, with the intent on working on the book. Which I did, surprisingly, until 11PM, which is the latest that I have stayed up in India. As I look down, I see I have written 13,314 words, equating to 42 pages, on this trip since arrival. I think I have another 25 or 30,000 words about the time period from January 6th, when I received the Wheels of Awakening invite, up until I left for India. I think there are another 25,000 words on the Gangotri trip which will be tacked onto the front of this book, so I feel like I have been making some serious headway.

Paul, Tom & Josh enjoying breakfast @ The Organic, the restaurant behind us

Nubra Valley, Ladakh, India

Thursday, September 11th, 2025

I have been in India for 11 days now, four days in Rishikesh and seven in the Himalayas, centered out of Leh in Ladakh. Five days of riding, bonding with my Royal Enfield. We are well past hump day, the mid-point in our journey. Not sure anyone wants it to end. After the giant work getting to the Highest Pass and beyond, everyone was ready for a day of peace and contemplation. Annemarie led a lovely yoga practice, all Kriya, in an area above our restaurant. It was beautiful with log ceiling and bright open windows letting in the cool Himalayan breeze. Breakfast was a slow and easy affair with stations for omelets, and crepes, tea, fruit and baked goods. Inside was the full buffet lay out. No one is missing any meals! They gave us the morning off until noon when there would be a Wisdom Talk at noon at The Organic! I retreated to my room to write.

At noon Anand-ji came over for a Wisdom Talk. He covered much, again based on questions from his flock. I managed one for him today. "Anand-ji, since I have been with you, you have changed the delivery make up of your Journeys. What was once a 50-50 mix of asana / Kriya, has morphed into a Kriya only Journey. Could you comment on that? Not that I miss the 3 minute planks to the 2 minute forearm planks to 3 minute full plank days!"

He said that he had shifted, but it depended on the classes. He himself is getting over asana and feels that what he wants to give to students is what will benefit them the most. Of course, as always, he went on for 15 or 20 minutes sharing his wisdom on a tangential level. The big bonus is the eye gazing with him when you are getting answered. Those deep, dark giant pools of love that are his eyes, letting you in and reaching inside me. You are engaging with your Guru Deva at a deep level, and it is sublime.

In that session he also said the greatest thing, which really was, for me, the highlight of all his words. "I don't like to teach to huge audiences. And I won't. I like the intimacy of a small gathering. Some people call me arrogant for that position, but I don't care, I really don't." This was always one of my biggest concerns, that one day I would come to Sattva and be one of a thousand. Oh, he will always be my Guru Deva, will always be with me. But when I am in India, I prefer those same small gatherings. That concern was permanently allayed as of today. I told my thoughts to Annemarie, who was sitting next to me for the talk this morning. Come to think of it, magic always happens when I am sitting next to the radiant Annemarie. I love her. Like the monks we see in the temples here, she has given up everything to have it all, in service of Anand-ji and each of us. Deep honor and respect for her.

Sam and my beloved Annemarie, Queen of Kriya, Princess of Sattva

We were told that today would be a total chill day, we could do whatever we wanted. We did need to get gas though, as a station was iffy on our longest drive tomorrow of 180 kilometers. Our bikes were still at the Anand-ji's hotel, so Graham, Floris, Henri and I decided to get a ride over there to retrieve our bikes and go fill up. As you might imagine, our comedy team took the wrong road from the start and drove along a dirt and gravel road in the valley by the river. It was flourishing with wildlife...horses, yaks and even camels. We can face to face with a shepherd(?) leading two camels along what, at this point, was a sand dune trail. They were immense creatures, giants humps and very, very wooly, to prepare them for the winter months. We passed what looked to be the start of a circus of some kind and would ask passing cars for directions to the station. We made it to the HP station and filled out tanks to the top.

The direct road back to the Organic Village Retreat was much quicker! Graham, ever my brother, and Floris, who I discovered was Duitch, and I had a little sangha. Him being Dutch is funny as my ex was also Dutch and I feel a real kinship with the country. I had been there maybe eight times in my president lookalike days and always had the best of times. Graham told a story about his true Soul Mate, a phrase not to be taken lightly in this instance. From Floris, we both learned about the world of osteopathy, of which he is a practitioner. Fascinating lunch. I shared with them some knowledge about my Sattva experiences and life on the campus.

Flavia, Floris and the crew resting upon approach to Pangong Lake

Right at the beginning of the trip, Adam, the film director, or as he noted, co-director with Ma, had told us that the crew would love some daily snippets, in landscape format, please, of anything we might like to record: be it spiritual, the trip, the beauty of the mountains, anything that would give them insights into our characters, should they decide to spend some time with us in the film. I had fallen down on that as I was dedicating such a large volume of my time to keeping this book up to date. But this afternoon, bright and sunny, I pulled a chair over by the clear creek that runs through the property and ripped off three clips. I will try to do better. With all the beautiful and interesting people here, I don't spend much time thinking about how much film time I will receive in the ten episodes. But I do feel I need to honor his request as he is such a consummate professional, a true believer in the Sattva and an all-around fine gentleman who I have come to care for greatly.

Rama, Adam and Scotty will bring you the cinematic story of our tribe's trip

I told him yesterday that every day until the film comes out that I will be praying for him. That Saraswati may sit on his shoulder and imbibe him with a clear, creative consciousness, that she helps with blockages on the creative process and brings as much divine knowledge to bear as he can effectively use to bring Anand-ji's gift of knowledge forward with the most clarity to the broadest audience. And that Lakshmi may sit on his other shoulder, paving the way as he negotiates for a distributor and does the marketing involved in making this film a huge success, worldwide. His success in this endeavor is my great prayer. It is why I am on this pilgrimage.

The evening brought the cultural presentation of Ladhki dancing and singing by five women from the Nubra village where the hotel was located. It was special as they also showcased their headdresses, resplendent with polished turquoise. The MC related about those being exceptionally valuable to the girls as they are handed down mother to daughter over the generations. It is one of their many links to their ancestors. I dwelled on the fact that turquoise is so valued by the Hopi, Navaho, and Apache tribes in Arizona. The dancing was not elaborate, Tahitian Hula like, but was simple hand movement and short steps with their feet, which were adorned with shoes that had the front end pointed and then rolled back.

The singing was in super high octave, typical of Tibet and many Oriental cultures. The girls really did belt it out though! Final dance was to involve the audience. When I heard that, I quickly exited the front row. After all, I left my rupees in the room, and they had a rather prominent tip box. I am not sure why, but whenever audience participation events happen, cast members make a bee line straight for me. In Gangotri, even the blind woman beggar managed to head straight for me in a scene of about a dozen pilgrims. When I returned, the whole group was up and dancing, so I was quickly all in on that. It was a joyous event that fitfully capped our two nights at the hotel.

Surprisingly, the yurt had a big, overstuffed, Naugahyde upholstered chair and ottoman. (I will miss my yurt!) I put my huge and thick Ladakhian blanket down and wrapped myself in it cocoon style and settled in for a couple of hours of writing. Before bed I completely packed, as it was a 7AM breakfast and 730 departure for the main hotel and an 8AM send off from there.

THE LONGEST RIDE...

TO PANGONG LAKE,
NEAR THE CHINESE FRONTIER
Friday, September 12th, 2025

After a yummy breakfast, again an omelet, 3 glasses of apricot juice and some fruit, we transitioned over to the main hotel. Most of my gentlemen friends here agreed that we were allowing ourselves to be overfed, so everyone was keeping it reasonably lite. Our group, our bikes and luggage all made it over the Stone Hedge Hotel for that 8AM leave, although departure ended up being 9:15ish. We are in the flow here, as all will attest. Take it as it comes! The governor hadn't left yet, and I am sure his guards were quite surprised by our assortment of yogi bikers.

Finally, after a big Love Circle in the garden at that hotel, Anand-ji took off...and headed right down the road we were on yesterday to get gas. The long cut way. Three people laid their bikes down in the sand before we made it to the gas station. No camels today though. Apparently, some people didn't get the message to fill up their bikes yesterday, so we had another pit stop while various tanks were filled in our delayed departure.

Anand-ji had announced at yesterday's Wisdom Talk that today's ride would be the longest of the trip. We would be crossing two 17,000+ foot passes and traveling over 240 kilometers. It was also the hardest ride. It is impossible to imagine how many turns I have accomplished on this journey, but I am pretty certain today's total surpassed the other five days combined. It was quite literally, for me, a full and complete, very hard workout. As I type at 830PM tonight, my big goal for the evening is going to be staying up until 930! My butt is sore, my lower back is sore, my hands are sore from gripping the handlebars. My head is sore from the piercing attention one needs to summon up to work the challenging roads. My neck is sore from the unnatural seating position. But you know what? I wouldn't trade this day for all the rocks in the Himalayas. It was stellar.

We headed back to the km101 Dhaba, turned left and then right on to an impossibly thin road that was a connector to the road to the Chang La pass. That road was basically empty of all traffic for miles and miles. Up, Up, Up. Switchback after switchback. After about two and a half hours of concentrated motoring we reached Chang La. 17,688 feet, so way up there.

Alice and Michel summiting Chang La!

We knew we were getting close as all the traffic started to snarl. Selfies, snowballs, pictures of the monuments, giant trucks, tourist vans and motorcycles. We spent about 15 minutes and then powered down the mountain towards what would be a coffee break spot...chai, tea, French Fries (of course) and fried cauliflower. About 5 klicks before stopping there, the rider in front of me went down. It was Ian. I pulled up to him, and he said he was ok and stood his bike up. I guess his tire was woefully underinflated and just let him down at the wrong moment. At the snack session, Omi, our traveling mechanic, had the tire off and was doing the repair.

It is seriously a true wonder of the world that all of our tires didn't suffer the same malaise. While the roads were the best in the world (Hi Five, BRO!), when they weren't, usually due to landslides, rockfalls or water crossing the river, they were exceptionally bad. Surely my tires met with more potholes than I have come across in my lifetime. Most bikes did not have even close to new tires. I had my rear end spin out a couple of times when crossing the road where water and sand had mixed. I don't like sand! And I don't like gravel! Especially on corners.

20km before the snack break, I had my biggest scare of the journey so far. I was going about 50 kph when out of the blue a dog bolted down a hillside and straight across the road. He was on a perfect trajectory to get T-Boned by me. It was looking to be a sure accident and a very bad situation for both of us. But as always, the gods were with me and shining down their protection. 18 inches from my wheel, the pooch was able to execute a 90 degree turn at full speed and avert disaster. It makes you think about what would happen if you hit a cow or, God forbid, a yak! Stay in the flow, find alignment with the silent mountains...

Anand-ji spoke at the snack session, telling us we all had to buck up, we still had another three or four hours to go and it would be hard work, just like what we had gone through. "You all know what you signed up for and all of you can dig deep and get it done." Oy...I thought we only had 50 kilometers to go, but that was far from the case. After a half hour in the bright sun and on the grass, it was time to go. First destination point, Warila Pass, a 17,429 footer. Push the repeat button. Switchbacks, curves, elevation and intensity. Up and over the pass without all of the hullabaloo of the other two, and over and down.

Tatia celebrating on Wari La Pass, 17,429 feet!

After about 90 minutes we were coming down the mountain, I was following Anand-ji (I thought it was Adam, they have the same grey helmet) and two giant Tata trucks heading up the twisty road were hogging the pavement. They were not about yielding, and four of us were just squeezing by. At that moment, my front tire shifted off the road into some soft dirt or sand and just as the back of the second truck went by, I became a member of the roll over club. I went down. I was only going about 3 kph so I kind of set the bike down and jumped out of the way so it wouldn't land on me. Two bikes stopped to help me lift it up as it was almost at a 100 degree angle to the road. These Royal Enfields aren't light. My old BMW 650 only weighed 436 pounds, 200 kg, and I could always retrieve it myself. These Himalayan 450s are closer to 550 pounds, 250 kg, I suspect. No damage to the bike other than some scratch marks on the roll bars...they did their job! And my left mirror a bit askew. No worries. Turns out we were stopping for another snack in just 3 kilometers. Of course, as soon as I stopped the bike, my Guru Deva was right there, inquiring about my spill and making sure I was OK.

Pride injured, being the biggest damage done, I motored the next three km where a coffee stop was planned. What cute coffee shop! They had baked goods and a full-on espresso machine. I got in line for a chocolate cake thing that had chocolate frosting and an actual Oreo cookie wedged onto the top. Unthinkable this for away from normal civilization! I waited 20 minutes in line while Graham, Gawita and Rodrigo ordered specialty coffees. Either the service was slow, or they were having difficulty clarifying their order, but I am not a stand line person, particularly in a coffee shop So I bolted out of there, went next door to the general store and got some peanuts, a small pack of cookies and some matches...I had brought a candle. I was out of the market in 30 seconds. That candle is shing brightly next to my laptop as I type away.

Soon Anand-ji gave the signal, and we were off on our final leg to Pangong Lake, elevation 14,100 feet, 4350 meters. And what a yummy desert it was after the long journey we had today. A beautiful, wide open, full-sized four lane road, exquisitely paved. Long sweeping curves easily rolled through in 4th or 5th gear, no sharp mountainous switchback curves. Such a pleasure. Anand-ji pulled over so we could enjoy the serenity of a group of wild horses grazing in the stream-fed grasses. As always, mountains on both sides and mountain ranges behind those, usually covered in snow and endless unseen ranges behind those.

Then, the deep blue glow of the lake started to appear. It got broader, bluer and vaster as we continued on. About 3 klicks further, the group pulled over on a high vista point, and we all dismounted and spent 15 minutes taking in the view of the lake, celebrating the bounty of nature.

Pangong Lake...and this wasn't even all of us!

Onward to the Misty Hills Cabins. From the outside, these looked like all the other accommodations in Pangong...kinda like converted shipping containers. We were up the hill from the lake and had a spectacular view...quiet, peaceful and serene. We had an arrival circle, and it was a big lovefest after our long trip. And then rooms were distributed. I was at the hotel where we had parked our bikes, for which I was grateful.

Paul was overjoyed to arrive at the lake

I walked in my room and such a surprise. A 4 ft by 8 ft Tibetan rug on the floor, and of all things, one on the couch also, just like the ones at the temples the monks sat on.

There on the wall was the indoor air handler of a mini split HVAC unit. Could it be? Well, no, they were used only in June-August. But big surprise! There was an electric blanket! First time in the mountains here. Someone suggested turning it on a half hour before going to bed, then turning it off when you retired. I liked that advice. I did not want to wake up to pee in a freezing room, completely soaked in sweat from the blanket. When I did wake up to pee, it was freezing in the room, and I grabbed the super thick blanket from the closet and threw it over the comforter. Worked just fine. I did, however, turn that electric blanket on for meditation in my bed the next morning!

Dinner that night had a whole bunch of tired yogis. But the conversation was lively, and as always here in the Ladakh region, the food was so good and very plentiful, as everywhere.

Pilgrimage to T'om

On the Royal Enfield Himalayan

Saturday, September 13th, 2025

It was a nice night, I got a good 8 hours and then snuggled deep into the covers for another half hour, before grabbing my long sleeve shirt, plugging in the electric blanket, and sitting in bed to get into my morning meditation. They announced that there would be walk down to the lake at 9AM this morning. I have learned, if nothing else, to be mindful of my body, listen to it, and not push it, especially at 14,000 feet. I knew I could easily walk down to the lake, but the walk back would surely be a struggle and could result in some altitude sickness. And I was doing so good. Why take it to the limit? I hated to miss Anand-ji speaking, but the price of entrance would be too high. I had a full day of high altitude biking upcoming today, including the 17,800 foot pass en route back to the Rewa Hotel in Leh. I could get my japa in instead.

As I was gazing off, Dr. Kirk came by, and we struck up a very lengthy and wonderful conversation. He, too, was listening to his body. We had much to talk about: guitars, King Trump, life of a physician these days and some of my journey. It was quite pleasant, and I took away the knowledge that I had been speaking to a great man. I told him a pediatric ophthalmologist was one of my life heroes after he performed two eye surgeries on my 3rd, daughter one when she was 14 months and another at two and a half.

The group came back, reporting that many of them went for a purification swim in the cold lake waters, joining others who had done it the night before. And there was Rodrigo, going into his room to get a towel to head back down and get a dip in before breakfast.

Breakfast here was delicious, maybe the best of the trip, 15,000 feet in the mountains. We all loved how the entire kitchen staff stood behind the warmers as we scooped out our repast. So friendly, stalwart Tibetans, truly genuine, beautiful men. As we were prepping to leave, I noticed that the men were also doing the housekeeping. We did not see a woman in sight at the Misty Hills cabins.

I think we were all sad to see the mighty, blue Pangong Lake fade away as well travelled on. I moved my bike up on the road to prepare for an easy departure. We then had a getaway circle, Anand-ji bringing us all into focus and grounding. Soon the roar of the day began. The first gift of Ma Nature was the wild horses on the road outbound.

The long, beautiful road back, returning to where our final coffee stop of the day yesterday happened. I love that road! We put some high kph miles on and rolled into Coffee Town again. Anand-ji had a coffee waiting for him from the advance cars, but everyone else took it as a coffee break after only 40 minutes of riding. Lord save me from my judging of people whose morning revolves around coffee! Trust me, I have most of the other vices but am free from that one. I could see there were other riders that didn't want a 40 minute stop and were ready to go. I asked the guide, where there any turns to the pass or was the road straight there? "Straight there", was the reply. I revved up my bike and about 7 of us roared off. I thought Adam was going to lead the early birds, but, surprisingly, out in front zoomed Anand-ji, who must have banged his coffee back quickly.

We were only 5 klicks out of town and on the windiest part of the road, and here came a 12 vehicle military convoy...wide vehicles on a super thin road. We either had to stop off on the sandy dirt adjacent to the paved road or try to manage riding it. I hate sand and gravel, so for most of the trucks, I stayed put. It was the same area where I went down earlier. No repeat of that!

We rode hard to reach the gas station about 40 kilometers away. We pulled in as the front pack, but it was apparent a long wait was in store. Magically, the pump that was servicing a big dump truck opened up and I was able to get gassed up quickly. I chatted it up with the service attendant. "Has everyone been treating you nice this morning?" I asked. "Yes, sir, where are you from?" "I am from the US." He looks at me and goes, "You like Trump?" I give him the thumbs down. Then, I asked him if he liked Modi. The response was silence, but the eyes revealed his true opinion.

All gassed up, it was time to leave for our repeat visit to Chang La Pass, 17,800 feet. At this point, the need for speed had completely abandoned me. Completely! I had conquered the world's most treacherous and crazy roads for days, now the end was near, and I would be able to go home all in one piece if I just took it easy. And I did.

We were about 10km from the summit, and I rounded a corner and saw a bike off the road, laid over and about 6 feet down the side of the hill (thankfully, not a gorge or ravine). I pulled over and saw that it was our beloved Torsten, unharmed, but it took 5 of us to pull the bike back up to the road. We stood it up and I saw that the left rear-view mirror was missing. No other apparent damage and the bike started right up. Torsten is a great and experienced rider, and I knew he was not pushing it after his first rollover. That was my signal to carry on.

The road got increasingly stunning with glorious snowcapped mountain ranges. I was able to take in more of it now that I was chilling out. In what seemed like no time at all, Chang La pass loomed. Much less action up there this time. Calm and serene. I hung out for a bit and chatted with some guys, talked with some local visitors, who wanted pictures of themselves and me by the Royal Enfield. Now there was about 80 km to go. Since I was on the Slow Path and did not want to get lost going into town finding the hotel, I decided to follow one of the Sattva cars. Inside were Tatia and Sarah. And so it was, an easy does it trip, down, down, down. Sarah is apparently chronicling the trip for a photo journal, so we had the enjoyment of stopping on three or four occasions along the way for her to get in shots of various monasteries along the way. Perfect. I was on the home stretch, I had proved myself a worthy rider in the Himalayas. Now I could just take it easy and come home to my beloved Kathlen all in one piece, abrasion and broken bone free.

Aussie Sarah impressed me with her notetaking during wisdom talks.

As we got closer to Leh, some of the nearby towns were having traffic issues, usually the results of military vehicular movements. The first stop was reasonably short, and I stayed behind the White Toyota SUV carrying my friends. The second hold up was interminable, and my butt was getting very sore. I watched as my fellow Sattvans on bikes split the lanes and coasted past. Hating to ever wait, especially on a bike, I asked the driver for directions and gave my farewells. Like all roads, this one poured right into the traffic circle near our hotel. Sadly, in my joy of arrival, I took the traffic circle exit incorrectly (left side riding messing with me) and had to go about a klick until I could U-turn and correct my error. In a half block I was pulling up the driveway into the Rewa Hotel.

A successful end to the challenge of a lifetime for me. It would be the last time I got on the bike on this trip. We were certainly guided by the cosmic consciousness the whole way. Ma and all the gods and goddesses, as well as Anand-ji's sublime radiance put a sheltering golden dome over each and every one of the riders and passengers, vehicle drivers and their car passengers. While there were probably ten in the "rollover club", not one drop of blood was shed nor was any bike suffering even minor damages. That is golden protection for a group our size, riding the in terrain we did, for as long as we rode. Om Shanti Shanti Shanti. Om Mane Padme Hum. Om Namah Shiviah.

We were all filled with joy & Ananda. My Teacher, forever in gratitude to him.

We all tumbled into the hotel at various times. Yes, I was ahead of many of the coffee drinkers! Dinner came and went, and Annmarie posted the schedule for schedule for tomorrow's busy day on the WhatsApp chat. My goal for after dinner was to once again manage to stay awake until 930PM. It was tough! But between talking with Kathleen and a little internet surfing, I managed it. Then came my best night of sleep on the Pilgrimage...9 straight hours.

Johnny & Melissa contemplating their hang gliding the next day

Exciting Day in Leh

Sunday, September 15th, 2025

Well, we all woke up in time for an 830 AM practice, led by, surprise, Michel! He did a fabulous job and offered up some Kriya and a bit of asana, with was much desired by all of us I feel. After all the riding, a little bending and stretching goes a long way. It truly started out the day in a perfect manner. We powered into the restaurant and had breakfast, preparing for a noon Wisdom Talk by Anand-ji.

We settled in for the Satsong. As always, Josh, Greg and Henri were stationed front and center:

We should expect to be thriving, living a full life. We are designed to have extraordinary experiences. And as we become more mature in our learning, we should expect that they happen increasingly.

We are living in a time of plenty. There is an acceleration in the field as the age of information and technology advances with lightning speed.

High / good energy is available everywhere, at all times.

Take note of the incredibly powerful gifts of Nature, use them when you can…wisely. Ayahuasca was used as an example.

You are a mature person when others can depend on you.

We cannot fight the play of reality.

Intentionality is extremely important in these times.

To be of seva is a part of maturing.

If we feel like the world or our relationships aren't giving us enough, it is because we don't feel like we have enough.

As always, the only way out is in.

Acknowledging that there is a part of our mind that is involuntary. Harness your mind through Kriya, study, meditation and practice and you will then be able to master your mind.

When you become rigid in your ways or outlook, you suffer. Go with the flow!

Your natural state is giving and the more you give the more you receive.

When Nature knocks on your door, follow! Now! Don't hesitate. All will unfold in ways that you cannot anticipate or understand.

Most of us skipped lunch as we knew we had a big dinner coming up. The plan was to visit the Shakti Stupa and then the Leh palace monastery. As I said, I had given up my motorcycle riding and was in a car for the first time in Ladakh. We motored through the city, and as always, up and up to the Stupa, which overlooks the city. It turns out much of it was funded by a Japanese Buddhist master and as you walk to the base, his name is sighted, and the Japanese lettering surrounds the Buddha relief.

Also noted was that His Holiness the 14th Dalai Lama set the cornerstone for the stupa. We discovered that His Holiness has a summer home in Ladakh and spent a month there this year. Our travel guide, Nuwang, told me he had a meeting with Him, arranged by his Buddhist Association in town. He glowed talking about it. The Dalai Lama has the entire state of Ladakh as his flock, and he ministers to them with his well-known compassion. I also talked with him about the 15th (potential future Dalai Lama) and how the Chinese were planning on taking over the role of choosing him. I said I was sure no one in Ladakh would follow the Chinese Dalai Lama, and he said, "No one." His Holiness has said recently that he might not oversee the picking of the 15th one, due to the Chinese influence. I personally entertain the notion that one will be found, and the monks will immediately take him into hiding for all the training needed, in a place safe from a Chinese kidnapping.

Anand-ji gave talks on the upper-reaches of the Stupa, giving us insight into the sacred Tibetan Buddhist ways. The view of the city was extraordinary, and we spent over an hour wandering clockwise around the monument.

It was time to go, and we worked our way across the city to the Leh palace and monastery. Like the Shakti Stupa, this overlooked the city, from another mountain, and was viewable from many areas. We parked in a zone that was resplendent with as many Tibetan prayer flags as you could ever imagine, all fluttering in the wind. The views of the mountains surrounding the city were stunning. I looked over at the steps to the monastery and said to myself, "I am going to be missing this one!". Too many and too steep. Then the thought entered that maybe I should push this one. I was doing fine keeping any altitude sickness at bay. I was glad I went up. In the monastery was another giant Buddha, but this one had the most electric, compassionate eyes of any of the temples we had been in. I sat with my mala and did 108 Om Mani Padme Oms. It felt really good. Further up the steps was another temple and Anand-ji was speaking outside. But the walkway was too narrow, and after my 108 mantras, I was one of the last up there.

Annemarie and I were talking about the powerful Tibetan Buddhist vibe that came from all these sacred spaces and how much we were thoroughly enjoying being immersed in it. I kept remembering Anand-ji's statement, "It is not the dogma or belief, but the energy from these sacred spaces." Energy indeed.

It was time for dinner, and all were hungry and filled with anticipation! An Italian restaurant, with a French name, Bon Appetit, in the Tibetan city of Leh. I told them my Sicilian girlfriend was looking for a full report! Again, we wove through the city streets until we stopped at a place where there was a sidewalk between two buildings and our guide motioned us down the path. 200 meters later, winding our way down, we entered the wooden gate of Bon Appetit! As we walked in the Ladakhian cultural entertainment had already begun on a large outside area. There were five ladies, dressed in the same outfits as at The Organic Village and singing and dancing in a similar manner. Difference was we had men also this time. They rotated through the men's and women's dances, then performed some numbers together. The big surprise was the dancing yak, managed by two men (maybe women?) who went around sniffing on many people. As normal, the ceremony ended with an all In dance! Everyone was laughing and having a good time.

The gods be with us; it was time to eat! We reassembled inside and I sat at a table with Paul and Dave. While a bit slow to begin, the food started to roll out. Ramesh and Ravi were called on to help wait tables. First came the cucumber and feta salad, followed by a green salad. Ummmm, so yummy. Then came four different pasta dishes intermingled with pizza. I am ashamed to say that the three of us managed to make five pizzas disappear. I am just going to right here blame Dave as the ringleader! Just when the gluttony got overwhelming, out came desert. Ours was apples and pomegranate seeds in a creamy pudding type base. We all groaned with delight. For me it was my first Western meal in two weeks, since the Andaz

Aerocity breakfast feedbag! Anand-ji was walking back to the hotel, and several went with him, but a number of us opted for cars.

We rolled into Rewa, and I headed straight to bed exhausted from another fulfilling day with Buddha and food. It was 830PM and I had another mission to stay up until 930PM again. I called Kathleen, told her all about the dinner, the pesto pizza, the mushroom cheese ones and the evening. She was satisfied they had taken good care of us! I wrote a bit and at 930, hit the hay. Interestingly enough, I had a huge potpourri of dreams that night, so many, and all completely crazy and totally unexplainable. I woke up more than a few times wondering what the heck was going on. In the end I slept to 630AM.

English Adam, Ian, Ganga Kim, Dave and Graham...each made my trip special.

LEH REGION BUDDHIST TEMPLES

Monday, September 15th, 2025

Today started with a Journey by Anand-ji and all of us were ready. Adam Shomer, sitting next to me uttered, "Oh Lord, here I am surrounded by these supremely talented yoga teachers. I can do this. I will do this!" (I later found out that he was joking, that he is a master yoga teacher and can keep up with the best!) I was thinking, I said those exact words on my first ever Journey with Anand-ji, three plus years ago, for my 200 hour training, We were mixed in with sixty 300 hour yogis, and I was intimidated. Subsequently, some of those 300 hour men and women became mentors and lifelong friends.

The room was quiet and contemplative as he walked in and started rubbing his palms. The three Oms. Then nadi shodhana, followed by a Kriya Love Liftoff. We did Cosmic Breath 7 for maybe 15 minutes and then he moved into Cosmic Breath 1 for 5 minutes. That led to us standing up and finding partners. I found out there was an odd number of us because I was left standing alone. Didn't phase me. Anand-ji would be my partner as well as everyone in the room. I wrapped my arms around them all in my mind. I found myself smiling broadly. In the background the guys who operate my tear ducts were preparing to go on strike for my overworking them. Tears ran down my face for 20 minutes, as was true for everyone. "Your life is a mandala! Celebrate it!" All of his wisdom and holiness came flooding out of him and open-hearted bliss was the only way I can describe it. When it ended, all around me people were kneeling, genuflecting and lying prostrate in front of our Guru Deva. All of this, through Kriya only, and with him, we moved mountains. The vibe in the post-class moments was as feel good as possible; everyone having poured out their hearts. We were spent yet completely fulfilled. We quietly and reverently made our way to breakfast.

Our final day in Leh and we were off to two more monasteries. All close by, an hour or so. First stop, the Hemis gompa, the wealthiest, most renowned and largest monastery in Ladakh. It was, indeed, impressive. First impression was an intricately engraved overhead gate, followed by a golden sided buildings with some beautiful golden relief Buddhas stamped into the metal. Mesmerizing! There were two temples many steps up...Buddha Temple and Main Temple. I was drawn to the Buddha Temple first above a large courtyard. It was fantastic with a giant brass Buddha overlooking the sacred space. How they got it there is a mystery, its weight being many tons, surely. I was as sublime as being in the spirit of the Buddha's presence gets. I pulled out my mala and did my six rounds of Lakshmi japa in this holy place. The Main Temple was seemingly much older and didn't hold my attention like the Buddha Temple.

I was totally stoked...the monks had a store here. I went in and found what I was looking for. The exact same kind of incense as I saw being burned in many of the temples. I picked up 6 boxes and a Buddha poster talking about it all starting from within, not without. Perfect. I checked out...1800 rupees. As I was walking out the door, there it was, on the wall, the one thing I had been looking for and could not find...a big, laminated map of Ladakh. OMG, only 150 rupees. Finally, I could get oriented and see exactly where we were, and more importantly where we had been. I had searched Amazon and Google for one and I'll be dammed if I could find one. And here it fell into my hands at the Hemis gompa, just like so many needs had when my luggage was a no show.

Gold relief Buddhas at the Hemis Gompa

We were off to our next stop, Thiksey Temple, again on the outskirts of Leh. We had passed it yesterday and had actually stopped in the lower parking lot for Sarah's photo chronicle. It was another vast monastery up on top of a local mountain. Today, we pulled into the upper lot, and I saw that people were tending to Torsten. I jumped out of the car to check on him! It seems like he was in his third defensive maneuver accident, but different result. This time his bike landed on his leg and twisted his ankle awkwardly. I knew he was devastated, not from the hurt, but from his third spill. I was riding in the car with English Adam, and we looked up at the numerous steps. He helped me find someone to offer a shoulder to get Torsten on his feet and up the first set of steps. As soon as our travel host saw us, she summoned a car to drive up and pick him up, getting him as close to the bottom steps of the monastery proper as possible. By the time I got the car, some other hardy souls got him up 50 more steps.

He didn't want to go further, having found himself a shady spot with a beautiful overlook of the sectioned off lands. Making sure he was AOK, I trudged on. I had thrown doubt to the wind and was now taking the steps as they came.

I removed my shoes and entered the main temple. I began the clockwise stroll around the temple proper and finally came face to face with a giant Buddha, who had been lowered down so really just his head was at eye level, right there, gazing at you with his caring, loving eyes. Somehow the Buddha had wings, exquisitely adorned that came up to the top of his head.

(A photo of this Buddha graces the front cover of the book)

I was stunned. I was on my knees in meditation position and began a round of 108 OM Mani Padme Hums. I felt as radiant as I ever was on this trip. I finished up and backed out of the temple, feeling Sri Buddha's serenity washing over my body.

This temple had a very special feature... a soft serve ice cream machine, served up by one of the monks. I ordered two, one for our lovely and able travel assistant guide, who expressed her gratitude. On the bench nearby were two monks enjoying the frostee freeze and I begged their permission to take a photo. It was a delight enjoyed by the majority of our group as well as many other temple visitors. Spiritual marketing! And a good price, too. Both for 150 rupees, about US$1.30. I helped Tosten down the many steps, although he did the one-legged hop most of the way until the car was there, waiting for us. I had a most lovely conversation with English Adam on the way home. We traded many stories, and I was proud of his full life of travel and adventure, something that eluded me at his age because of two daughters, love them that I did.

As we pulled into Leh, our driver surprised the hell out of us by playing his country and western mix. At the entrance to Reyn, he was playing Chris Stapleton's "Tennessee Whiskey"! I am sure Sattva country star Courtney will get a kick out of that! Adam and I sure did. We flowed into the hotel to be told that dinner was at 730PM. Oh my, a three hour plus break. I used all of it up in my room, working on the book. It was a relief as I got completely caught up to the minute.

You never know when synchronicity is going to hit. At dinner I enjoyed having a lovely talk with the woman seated next to me, that I hadn't spent much time with, Sandra Valenta. She told me she and her hubby flew non-stop Air India ORD to DEL. I was interested, as the airline has me scratching my head as so many of my travel blogs give it scathing reviews. She gave a common assessment of her business class experience, lovely service, but an older plane. Well one thing led to another, and it turned out they live in Wauwatosa, Wisconsin! This is where both of my parents grew up and went to high school! We had lots of stories to trade.

Now it is 940PM and I made my target stay up time. Up early tomorrow and we will leave the hotel at 7AM for our flight to Delhi and on to Dehradun, close to Rishikesh. What an adventure. What a pilgrimage what a time of our lives.

Flying to Sattva in the Flow

Tuesday, September 16th, 2025

*W*ell now, where to start. For me, it is back to the beginning, but here is how it unfolded.

We left for Leh airport on schedule @ 7AM. This time we had two buses as well as our cars. I rode in a bus; the truck held all overflow luggage. We got to the airport, and it was kind of India craziness. We pulled our luggage off the truck and headed to the initial check in line. Torsten passed me lying on a baggage cart! When we got through the check point, I shouted to Danny, who was with him, that there was a wheelchair up there to the right. In he went.

Then there was the Xray of the bags, which went fairly smooth, and I was OK'd to move into the check in area. There was a lady doing boarding passes at a kiosk and I thought sure, do it. Got my passes and got in line for bag drop. The line didn't move. Then a new line opened for business class. I bolted, and waited, but finally got to the counter. Trying to avoid baggage fees I asked about an upgrade. Shockingly, the upgrade to premium economy was only 1100 rupees. I said, "Sign me up"! Then he said no discount or perks on the bag fees, though. Unfortunately, he said to go with this lady to pay. Apparently, LEH did not let customer service agents take payment. OK.

I follow the woman to an off the way office, on airside of security though. And there was Adam Shomer paying for his excessive baggage fees. Anand-ji was there for same. Shortly, over a dozen of our tribe joined outside the office, which was something you might see in Midnight Express before being carted to off to the brig. Adam finished up and hurried off. Anand-ji insisted I sit down before him, his beautiful loving self, and I took a chair with the lady. She proceeded to hand me off to a guy and it began. 20 minutes later he could not maneuver the 2010 era software make it happen, so I said cancel that request and just let me pay 4kg overweight baggage fee. Another 20 minutes. During this time I started chanting OM Mani Padme Hum. I probably got through over 360 of the mantras before "Bing" my 2740 rupee fee posted. There was frustration in the line outside, it was obvious some were not going to be able to pay their fee on time. I left the office, Anand-ji had left ten minutes ago, and Sam took his place. Like me, she had huge frustrations, but we acknowledged and rode the flow.

I went back out to the check in counter and it turned out they didn't even weigh my bag, but for some reason put the business red tag on the luggage. He printed my ticket, and I saw I had a premium economy seat without paying for it. That was special. In the end, the flight was delayed by about 90 minutes. As we went through the boarding process, Torsten rolled by me in a proper wheelchair and they pushed him out on the flight ribbon and rolled him 200 yards to the plane. We all took buses to the plane. Oh India!

The boarding process took at least 60 minutes, so I was thrilled to have more legroom. I was sitting next to Ganga (Kim) and we had a lovely chat. Finally, we took off to Delhi. Apparently, they were holding our Dehradun flight for us, which was great. We landed and exited the flight, down the long concourse, through a couple of security checks, even though we came off of a domestic flight. Anand-ji had new boarding passes for us and eventually we made it to gate 29B at Terminal three. On the plane we went, and this process went smoother! Up in the air to our final location. There were two babies in front of us and they didn't make a peep. For a 20 minute flight they served, and cleaned up, a box lunch. We landed and fetched our bags. In the US, we don't get a meal on a 90 minute flight.

We were 2.5 hours behind schedule. At baggage claim, Jemina made The Big Announcement. The storms had washed out the road to Sattva and Ramesh had booked us lunch at a lovely hotel in Tapovan, outside of Rishikesh. On the way to the hotel, I told my seatmates on the bus there that we would be staying the night in town, almost for sure. I took out my mala and did 12 Om Shrim Lakshmiya Namaha rounds, as I had missed a day on the motorcycle tour. The staff had found a great hotel for lunch and at during our repast Anand-ji made Another Big Announcement. The road to Satttva was scheduled to open at 9PM tonight, and that might be iffy. He had decided we would stay in town. I figured this was coming and was thrilled that I was given a room at the same hotel as lunch. I had to climb the exterior bus ladder and point out my bags on the roof and haul them in.

AT 6PM I rode the elevator to my 2nd floor room. Lovely room. Cool, on the corner, so lots of windows. Truly bad internet, but my Verizon was working here on my cell phone, unlike in Ladakh, so I would be able to communicate with Kathleen and get any group WhatsApp updates.

So, we left the Leh Reyn hotel at 7AM and checked in at Tapovan at 6PM. 11 hours! Same amount of time as my flight from Tucson to Dallas (normally 90 minutes), that started my jumbled, lost bag, travel experience back on August 30th.

The crew at The Palm Bliss, still smiling despite the delays!

TRYING FOR SATTVA AGAIN!

Wednesday, September 17th, 2025

Woke up and repacked. I brought my luggage downstairs to beat the elevator jam up. Breakfast was at 7:30, and at 9AM we were heading out to Sattva, at last. The road was reported as open and off rolled the buses with the tribe who had stayed our hotel, one of three.

We shortly crossed the Ma Ganga bridge with the Sattva billboard (called a hoarding in India) for travelers going the other way, and a new Rasa Hotel billboard for us heading up to Sattva. We wanted to turn left at the Garuda temple, but our bus was stopped. The road couldn't yet handle tour buses of our size, only sedans and motorbikes.

At this point, nothing fazed us. We took it in stride. There were three or four chai / snack shops there...we would be AOK. To join us we had the regular brown monkeys and then a pack of long-tailed, white head monkeys showed up and they are the alphas. The browns faded away. They were on top of the tourist vans in no time, checking to see if they could get into any bags stowed up there...no luck! We had a bus full of pilgrims; all dressed in light lavender saris and robes pull up with us. They were traveling with their guru and were in the same situation as us. They had long, almost African style bindis on their heads and they were exotic bunch.

Another bus load was a younger crew and they were fun. They were knocking off some Bollywood moves in the street, and encouraged us to join in. Henry and Ganga took them up on it and soon there was fun dancing in the streets. Only in India!

The road closure meant Sattva would have to organize cars to pick up all the people and luggage. Paul T saw the film team pull up from the city in a sedan and made his move to jump in with them. Good move, Paul!

The Garuda Temple

Soon I saw the shopkeeper for Sattva come down in his car and I jumped in. We were off, after an hour's wait.

The road was as bad as I had seen it in six years. Trees down, big landslides, water gushing over the road in many spots. I was getting anxious about our odds for tomorrow's departure. I thought about staying in Tapovan as a back-up, my outbound flight to Delhi nightmare still lingering in my brain. At this point though, I was more than completely in the flow and basically said "fuck it!", I am going to go to the campus and what will be, will be. Of course, I wanted to be a part of the closing ceremony. I couldn't remember for the life of me what I had left in my room when we departed so many days ago for Ladakh.

Probably the worst spot on the road for the cars was at the small stores in Mohan Chatti village, just before the Sattva driveway. There was a small river flowing across the road and it had undermined a bunch of concrete. Our Suzuki sedan got to enjoy two loud bangs on the undercarriage as it went over the 10" high crack in the road. We all grimaced. But in 30 seconds, we were turning right into the Sattva driveway. Despite all the obstacles of the last two days, here we were! Home!

I headed straight to the office to see if my room was open. I had forgotten my room number (this getting old is really a mixed blessing) and opened the door to a fresh and clean, freezing room. I had really left virtually nothing in the room, because I came with nothing...only the two shirts and two pants which had made it four days til I went to Delhi to retrieve my suitcase. Oh, and there was the bald eagle feather that I intended to plant on the highest pass. (Turns out that it had a far better destiny). I dove into the shower.

I could look out my window and see that the others were arriving, and Annemarie notified us there would be a Satsong at 1:30. Good! I was ready for it. Before it started, I had a lovely Dharmic chat with Leanne.

Right off the bat, Anand-ji says, "Don't let everything be a big deal…FLOW." How long will the radiance last or will the habit energy take over? Continuing…

- When our Nature comes through, we can handle anything!
- The is nothing Big in life, only this moment. How do you show up? People want to have great life but can't have a great moment.
- The goal of a teacher is to lead you to you.
- In the end, we have all gotten here, but what will you do now? *(Beloveds, this is a statement that has been recurring to me over and over…Here we are, all that we have been through together, all that you have seen and learned. All of the exposure you have had to the Sattva life with Journeys and Wisdom talks. Are you going to let habit energy take over? Or are you going to begin a deeper dig? Are you going to sign up for SattvaConnect so you can stay close to the teaching, practice yoga with Sattva master teachers and enjoy Anand-ji's many talks for the past five or ten years? Some have said they are going to sign up for teacher training or already had. Rhonda is going for Masters training in January! I salute and honor that because she and the others are growing, evolving and transcending. They are ready to do the work now that they have seen the light. I truly, from the bottom of my heart, pray that each and every one on this journey will look deep and find the desire to continue down the Dharmic Highway with Anand-ji).*
- In life, there is no OFF button, only ON.
- In space there is no boundaries, In life, you make your walls. Step into your infinite life. Always try to step into your higher self, not your habituated self (karma).
- Find freedom from the compulsion of being your lowest self. Freedom is an inside job!

- Disengage from the addiction of being your tiny little self. Choose freedom. Infinite freedom of existence is yours for the taking.
- Only you hold the keys to releasing yourself from the prison of gloom. Use them to open the door to bliss.
- Don't be consistent in the habit of being yourself.

When the final talk was over Anand-ji decided that we would have the closing ceremony at 5PM, instead of the traditional morning on the day of departure. Great! I went and scheduled a 90 minute massage for 7PM. That felt like it would be heaven after so long on the bike. The fire ceremony will surely be over by then. After the wisdom talk, I took a nap. Then I unloaded my bags from Leh and repacked for the long journey home. A lot of dirty clothes! That was when I realized I had left 4 pair of linen pants and 3 kurta (the long, knee length men's Indian dress shirts) at the Reyn hotel in Ladakh. I had put them on the top shelf of the closet to keep them unwrinkled. I guess Ma India felt someone needed them more than me. Oh well, guess I wouldn't be wearing all white for the fire ceremony. I was into the flow of acceptance fully by this point. Everything has a reason, flow with it, no regrets.

I went down my 42 steps to the sidewalk and out to the Havana. It was brand new, and they had finished roofing it while we were gone. I was proud for all of us that we were inaugurating it...that honor would stand for a long time. After many of these ceremonies, I knew that my hot blooded, bad self was not a front row guy. I needed third row seating! Another benefit, former benefit it turned out, was not having samagri filling my hair and clothes. I say former, because this time the people in the 3rd row got two bowls, one filled with samagri and one empty, and we were to move the seeds from one bowl to another on the SwaHa!. Then at the end of the ceremony we toss in what we had. It was a great solution! Nonetheless, I was completely drenched from sweat by the end. I asked Anand-ji why he and I were such heavy sweaters, and he said, "It is Shakti, T'Om." And smiled broadly. I liked that answer a lot!

It was time for a chai break and then we headed over to Shiva Hall for a time when everyone could address the group as they would. I certainly had not planned for that final event when I booked my massage...I am pretty sure we had not had one like it before. I looked at my phone...I had 20 minutes until my massage started. I hated the thought of canceling that as there were no other openings that night and tomorrow would be crunch getaway time. It started with a few folks giving their testimonials and I went about 5th. I was grateful that Anand-ji was in the very back of the room, as my comments would be directed at him.

You see, dear tribe, what had surfaced for me during the ride, quite clearly, was that this would be my last trip to India. I felt like Anand-ji had given me so much and I knew I could continue on with my spiritual life with all the knowledge he had shared with me over the past 40 months. So, I spoke these words…

"Guru Deva, Loving Father, Beloved Son (he was staring intently at me) you have given me the world. You have taught me to Love, to have compassion, humility, opened the doors of the spiritual world for me. You have supplied me with all the tools I could ever want to continue my practice, my knowledge base, and to grow, evolve and transcend. My gratitude is so deep. As Sri Yukteswar said to Yogananda, every student must leave the sheltering wing of his teacher, I feel that I am now ready to fly from the nest, continue teaching and live my life to its final completion. I know that you will always be here for me, and I can assure you I will always be your loving chela, even if remotely."

"In honor of my flight from your loving nest, I have for you a sacred feather from the king bird of all birds in North America, the great Bald Eagle. This feather was collected on sacred Apache Indian land and has been treasured by Native Americans for millennium. I hope you can find use for it."

"I love you, Guru Deva, and the Gift you have given me is beyond compare. You have made me a True and Complete Man. I came to Sattva as a baby for my 200 hour and together you brought me through my 300 and Masters, as well as three sacred pilgrimages. I am a man in full now."

I imagine that the pronouncement was quite surprising to many. After a few more speakers, I had to leave for my massage. I walked up to Anand-ji and we hugged each other long and hard. It told him I wanted to make room for youth. He nodded.

And out the door I walked, which, in itself, surprised a few people who might have noticed. The massage beckoned and it was truly fantastic. Any toxins that were left after the yagya and the moto trip were ironed out. I struggled to stay awake on the table, even though it was a deep tissue style and I keep saying, go as hard and deep as you want. He is so pro and great. Then into the steam room…bliss. And out the door. I walked over to the café after about 110 minutes in the care of the spa…and no one was around! Shit! They had eaten dinner, and all gone to bed. The kitchen boss said, nope, they were all still in Shiva Hall. WOW! That was some serious testimonial offerings. I went back in and caught the last six or so speakers and was glad I did. Peter unable to speak, but wanting to touch everyone, walking around the room. Jen, eloquent, as always. My beloved Pennie speaking from her pure heart. Leanne, a lovely talk, even thanking those riders who carried her through the mountains (including me for two days). Despite Anand-ji's departure everyone was still going, right to the last person. And then a late dinner. It was a day and night to remember

I got back to my room and was packed and ready for tomorrow's departure. I wanted nothing to get in the way. I have long ago given up using the words I, me or mine in my prayers, so I prayed for all the others who needed to use the road for one reason or another. Other Sattvans were also leaving tomorrow. I did pray for sunny skies when I woke up!

INDIRA GANDHI INTERNATIONAL AIRPORT?

Thursday, September 18th, 2025

I slept hard, thought I head thunderstorms and just kept sleeping... I must have been dreaming. When I climbed out of bed and opened the curtains, there were two monkeys on my deck, wrestling away with each other. When they saw me, they both jumped at the glass door and scared the bejesus out of me. Welcome to the day! That's when I realized it had been, and was currently, raining. I don't know for how long, but I found out later that it was going on for 5 hours.

Go with the flow T'Om. Nothing can stop you now, you are going find comfort in whatever happens, because I am the creator! The Journey had been moved to an unthinkable 8AM. It would be my final live Journey with my Teacher. I was ready. Well...so was he! He absolutely ripped it. Very active, Kriya after Kriya. Arms up in ego conqueror for 5 minutes. A series of SO HATS that was kicking all of us. It went on. It was tough, it was deep, he wanted it to be something to remember. Of course, we were all drenched in sweat when he busted into the first asana I had seen him do in a long time. 20 down dog to plank to down dog, then 15, then 10. I wasn't going to be broken. Not a chance. I stayed with it, every Kriya, every breath hold, I ripped my chest open to glow and radiate, as he was bellowing for us to do. Then came the stand-up command. A few more Kriya and I knew what was coming...as he always does on the last Journey..."Let's Dance!" We spent 10 to fifteen minutes dancing around the room. After the serious workout, everyone had the energy to dance. And them, "Come up and gather together around the front."

This was it, my history of being present on campus was just about over. He spoke loving and encouraging words. As his talk ended, I got a good, long loving stare and smile from him. And Om Shanti Shanti Shanti Hari OM Tat Sat. I was in padmasana and bowed my head to the floor, deeply and for a long time filled with Bhakti Love and reverence for my Guru Deva.

After the Journey, I spoke with him again. I wanted to make sure he understood my decision and how grateful I was to him for EVERYTHING. Now I feel a little foolish, because of course he understands my decision, probably understood it from the moment I walked on campus on September 1st. Sometime his all-knowing self is beyond comprehension. Tomas' wife Regina has been instrumental in helping me understand. "You have to listen, T'Om, to his every word, every sentence. Each one has such infinite meaning, and he doesn't just speak to hear himself, he speaks to help us learn. He knows and understands so much." She has been with Anand-ji longer than any other person currently on campus and I take everything she says as saddled with a great deal of truth.

And those were to be the last words with my Great Teacher, at least in person. Of course, I can always meet him in the ethers, and if he wants me to know something, or has need of my seva in any way, I will sense that in meditation, or even while looking at the desert moon.

With the great illumination and radiance coming out of the Journey, the rain stopped and the sun poked through. All was well. I walked to the office to pay my bill and bid Ramesh and the office staff a hearty farewell. I put a $100 bill in the tip jar. They were always so kind to me and I felt like family immediately. I was sad I couldn't find Manoj to say goodbye. What work he does!

Leanne was kind enough to offer me a Sattva moto tee shirt as a gift. Of course, I had every intent of going into the boutique and buying that same shirt. I did go in later and exchange it for one size larger. I will think of her and our times on the Royal Enfield every time I wear it. I handed out a copy of my book to some people who were close to me on the trip....Jen, Rhonda, Leanne and Cory, whose significant other, Elena, I had done my 200 with, as well as Gangotri. A very special woman. Close to my heart. Jen gave me a copy of her hot off the presses new book, "Atlas for Lost Souls", which I will treasure and read on my long trip home to Tucson and Kathleen's loving arms.

Pennie, the angel hovering over the entire pilgrimage.

I had some last words in Rasa café with Sophie, and Graham gave me an encore performance of the poem he read last night, which I missed due to my massage. Touching. I told him I was going to call the BBC and see if he could audition for Richard Attenborough's job when he finally retires. The car and Pennie arrived; we dove in and were ready for the drive to Delhi.

Pulling out of Sattva was done with gratitude for the abundance of grace that had put me on the path to come there. Shockingly, I didn't cry.

The seven hour drive followed, the slowest driver I ever had from Sattva. I didn't care; we left 16 hours before my departure time on Qatar Airlines. We also stopped in Tapovan to do a little shopping, and I was blessed beyond anything to have my wonderful and dear friend from my 300, Krista, from Perth, suss me out before I left. We hugged hard and long. Lovely Krista (along with my beloved Courtney Cole) was the one whose push of confidence put me over the line for Master training in 2024. As it turned out, she could not make it, which was a sad day for me when I found out. She was there in January 2025 though. Courtney showed though and we have been joined together ever since.

Our driver stopped at the most divey dhaba I had ever been to on the long Delhi road. Pennie didn't even eat. I had two Special Lassies, which had cashews in them. Yummy. My trip with the gifted and enlightened Pennie will be one I shall never forget. We traded stories the whole way down, although mine paled into insignificance compared to her long and lengthy yogic history. The world is a special place with her walking around and being with her for seven hours made my life much fuller. I just love that girl. And special she is...we dropped her off at the JW Marriott so she could go to the spa there and get rubbed down and steam out the Delhi smog before her trip to France, where she would a week later lead one of her scores of retreats in the Cosmic Consciousness.

I got to Indira Gandhi 4 hours before the check in counter opened, thrilled out of my mind that the road from Sattva was open, we had clear sailing and, despite the start of my trip to India, things went smooth as silk. While standing in line there was a monk. I asked him if he spoke English and he winked and said that he gets by. Further conversation unfolded and he, in fact, worked at a temple in San Francisco and had seva as an outreach program for poor people who needed repairs on their house. I told him that I learned on my pilgrimage that the monks (and lay people) were praying every day for the welfare of all the people of the world. It was a lovely conversation and the commitment and joy of the Tibetan Buddhists, shall ride on my shoulders til I leave my body. How proud His Holiness must be of his monks and his flock. Truly some of the most beautiful people on the planet.

I am now in the Qatar business class club finishing up this final day writing and review. It is actually 1:20 AM…my flights leaves at 3:25 PM, to Doha, connecting to the Jordanian Air flight to Amman and on to Chicago, where I will spend the night and fly home on the following day.

THE LAST LEG AS INTEGRATION BEGINS

Saturday, September 19th, 2025

I am still going strong at 2AM, somehow, the latest I have stayed up in over a decade. At 2:30 AM, I leave the Encalme Prive Club and head to the gate. There were some electric cars waiting when I exited the elevator and I though, OK, let's do it...I've been up for 21+ hours. So happy I did, my gate was maybe a mile away. The driver kept going and going. I was thrilled to be riding, I gave him a tip, using up some of my remaining rupees, and got into the business class line.

The Qatar Air flight was as sublime as one hears, but I missed most of the 3 hour flight to Doha, Qatar, as I flattened out the seat and slept the whole way. Groggy, I stumbled out of the plane; to discover we had landed at the farthest gate from yet another security check. It was hot and I got to sweating again on the walk. Check in for the Royal Jordanian flight was smooth, but, poor, poor me, the Doha to Amman flight, while business, did not lot have a lay flat seat. Whine on, T'Om.

Amman was an older airport, nothing like the shiny showcases that are Doha and Dubai. Long walk again and strolled over, after the de riguer security check, to check in for my 13 hour flight to Chicgao. These were proper lay flat seats! My guy sitting adjacent to me was Syrian, and regaled me with photos of Damascus, with people partying at outside venues until late like in Capri or Mykonos. He said I just have to go, the celebrations after Assad fled to Russia were serious and ongoing. Maybe someday... As always, I watched over 5 hours of TV and slept for the other eight. We landed 45 minutes early.

We were off the flight first and the race was on for immigration. Half way there our group merged with a planeful of folks coming off a Qatar flight and I imagined the swarming masses at the stations.

I had used the MPC arrival software for internation arrivals, most thankfully. Coming into the large arrivals hall, it was packed! But there it was…a queue marked MPC. I followed it and it led me to an empty queue, one that planted me right at an immigration officer, with no one in front of me. My traveling misery had become traveling mercies! I popped out with no issues and there were my bags coming off the carousel. Om Shanti, Shanti, Shanti!

Caught the shuttle to the Hyatt Regency, where a 1200 sq foot, two story suite awaited me, courtesy of Oscar, my car dealer, yoga teaching, brother, who had arranged the room upgrade for me. Only one last hurdle. DFW had cancelled or delayed 1000 flights today and if my plane departing from Chicago to Tucson originated in Dallas, I would be trashed. I checked my favorite plane itinerary software, flightaware.com, in the morning and saw my flight was on schedule. I the checked on the incoming flight I would be using, and all the gods were with me!!! It was already in the air, from Miami! I would be getting home to the arms of Kathleen and Koko on schedule, most likely with my luggage, which I personally rechecked into American yesterday.

I am quite anxious to get back to Tucson and my small nuclear family. I am ready to integrate, begin my routine again of meditation, japa and a yoga class with St. Karen. And begin my study with be the Devas. The joy of my Lakshmi japa was going to know unfold into a deeper knowledge, study and familiarization of Saraswati and Kali. I was determined to continue to grow, evolve and transcend, as Anand-ji says, it is what Nature calls for.

*T*UCSON HOME

AND AFTERMATH THOUGHTS

*A*s always, I was welcomed at the Tucson airport by Kathy pulling up to the arrivals curb, Koko's head sticking out the window ready to see Papa. It was hot, a 100 degrees, but I was home. This journey took a lot out of me and much of the time in India I was just spent…pooped. The outbound travel nightmare pulled a lot of energy out of me, even though I did not let my guard down in dealing with the missing luggage. And in the end, I was fine! The detachment from my bag carrying my riding gear and cold weather clothes was a challenge that was met head on. As noted, I ended up having everything I needed and, what I didn't have, it was made available to me.

The trip home was almost 48 hours of travel, and while I was in comfort, it was a long, tough travel experience. Due to all of the disruption with flights, and layovers, I thought I was going to beat Mr. Jet Lag. But that is much easier said than done with 12 time zones to overcome. The waves of lag would hit me like a brick, stop me in my tracks or send me nodding off at my desk or on the couch. I have a follow up with my doctor tomorrow and then we pile into both cars and head up to the summer house for 10 days before we close it down for 6 months. It will be cool and refreshing 6300 feet up in the Arizona mountains, windows open at night.

As my trip unfolded in the end, the home thing was really resonating strongly with me. I just came to the realization that now, I have done it all. My dream of dreams, the Wheels of

Awakening trip was complete, and I was feeling like I have done it all. I have nothing left to prove. Now I could fully, completely and totally be at rest, retired and at one with where I was at...full retirement. Bliss from just sitting on the deck watching the pines grow, the elk wander through, the ravens fly by and stop trying to catch up with the world.

Yes, I am a complete man. I came into Sattva as a complete newborn, with a strong longing, but unsure what I was longing for. In forty months, Anand-ji changed my life. Yes, there was yeoman's work on my part, not to mention Tomas, St. Karen, Annemarie and Jemina's, but I have been shot out of the golden cannon of Sattva with wings to play out my life in full. As I go over and over my decision to use those wings to fly out of the sheltering nest of the campus, many things come to bear.

If I was going to divinity school to learn to be a pastor, would I stay on the campus forever? No, I would graduate (in my case as a Master Yoga Teacher) and bring what I have learned to the world. And that is exactly what I am doing.

I am not leaving Anand-ji or Sattva. How could I ever do that? I will be a lifetime alumnus! I have SattvaConnect.com with which to stay tight. I will be able to see my Guru Deva online and participate in the live feeds.

Anand-ji will be traveling! I heard he is thinking about the US every couple of years. I will be there!

There are the scores of people who joined me in one or all of my classes at Sattva who will stay in my life forever. Same with the pilgrims on the three pilgrimages.

I would just like to state and affirm that My Teacher has done his job! He has gifted me The Path, given me the tools with which I can continue down it. I have a clear and completely transparent view of how my life will play out. Would returning to India make me spiritually richer and accelerate all my learnings...certainly. But I now feel that the price in separation from my loved ones, on my body from jet lag, and my retirement fixed income pocketbook would all tug at me saying, "You have enough! Seven trips to India! Your Guru knows who you are and understands you deeply. Breathe! Everything you need is at your fingertips."

As I tried to document in my first book, my whole life was built, created and focused directly to the miracle of the last 40 months. All of it pointed to me finding Anand-ji, his teachings and his wisdom. It all happened and came into focus. Now I can take all that learning and illuminate it to my world. Open my heart in seva and share. Give.

As noted, one of the HUGE surprises was the male/female ratio for the trip. While completely unique to all my Sattva experiences, it took a bit of time on this trip for me to truly come to grips with it. All my life since 1970, when I graduated from Mercer Island High School, my best friends have always been women. I really had a very limited amount of guy friends in the subsequent 55 years. This is aside from my wives and girlfriends. I don't know why that is and perhaps Freud or Jung could work out the reasons. But here and now, it was bro time!

I was overjoyed when Dave reached out and said he was traveling the USA, working to get to the east coast for his November flight to India for a six month pilgrimage in the path of his guru, Yogananda. What a fun time we had hanging out, recounting the trip, and chillin'. I took him on the Finger Rock trail hike in my backyard. We rocked it to the highest point I have ever been to, 4509 feet from my home at 3100 feet. We left at 6AM and worked it until 930, when Kathy greeted us with fried eggs on bagels covered with some white cheese. Bro time, very meaningful to me. We enjoyed a great Greek dinner out and then hosted a small fiesta his honor, where I had local friends over, a chicken and steak BBQ, followed by a homemade blueberry buckle desert from Kathy's loving hands.

Many of the women had commented on how nice it was to have so many men in the group, being vulnerable and open their hearts. I wholeheartedly agree. It was one of the shining things that stood out to me. I very much enjoyed my discussions with Dave, Graham, Josh, Adam and Cory. There were so many stories.

On that same note, my sherpa's hat is completely off and I bow low to the women riders on this trip. Courageous, strong Warriors. I was in awe of their motorcycle riding skills and when we were deep in the mountains, I would love to watch one of the girls zoom by me. I haven't run across that very often in my bike career, if ever.

Also, to the women who summoned up the courage to ride on the back of a bike. These were twisty, thin roads here and yet, they offered up themselves to riders without concern here in the Himalayas. I love that, as I am not sure I myself would have jumped into the seat of someone I didn't know and zoom, zoom, zoom around the Himalayas! To their credit, Jen, Leanne and Rhonda did just that on the back of my Royal Enfield. I treated them all as the most special of VIP packages, marked fragile, despite their strong and Warrior spirits.

Speaking of the ladies, one of my first calls was to C, my esteemed yoga student who was waiting until this week (post-Lake Maggiore Italian wedding of her son) to tell her family about her breast cancer. She told me the reveal went wonderfully. They all understood why she didn't tell them prior, and they were proud to the ceiling that their mom / wife was handling the whole thing in such a beautiful, optimistic way. They could tell she was glowing. Oh, the rare person that glows when breast cancer rears its ugly head! As I said, she had absorbed all the teachings I had given her, rose above my status to become her own teacher / creator and was putting the knowledge to the correct use, with solid conviction. She knew that this was her life and while she could do nothing to control it, what would unfold would be a gift, just like every moment of her life.

She had told me that her Durga mantra was working wonders in my absence to India. She had found her perfect surgeon, more perfect than her previous one, who was not only an oncology surgeon, but also a plastic surgeon. So, whatever had to be done, full mastectomy or partial, she would be fixed up in the finest of ways.

When she talked about all of it, it was as if she was going to a garden party. So complete was her knowledge in the fact that whatever the outcome was to be, it would be the perfect outcome. Sweet Lord, my seva in teaching her had unfolded into the greatest satisfaction of my yoga career. I cried tears of joy when the call was over.

Post surgery, she had a fantastic surgical experience. She is now cancer free, healing rapidly without excessive pain, and continuing to live the Dharmic life.

My other triumph was in meeting a woman in our Tucson neighborhood, who also had a home in Durango, Colorado. I asked her to join me in a class at a local studio, which led to an ongoing dialogue. She subsequently bought and finished my book and decided that she needed more of this Sattva yoga life. I turned her on to Bill (yes, the Bill from our trip) in her Durango homeland and he has been doing Kriya work with her. She will be doing her 300 hour at Sattva in November. This will be my spiritual gift to her for loving my book so much! She will be a perfect yogi.

Oh yes, many of the conversations with everyone seemed to be about us being so "overfed" every step of the way. I came back to my Lila life having lost five kilos. How it happened, I don't know. Maybe the overhydrating. My weight was one of my focus goals back in January, a goal that was not met. Amazingly it was realized at the end of the trip after 2 weeks in the bosom of Tibetan Ladakh!

I am really not charmed by getting on any more airplanes and now have certainly passed the two and a half million miles of actual flight at this point. That was my old life. Granted we do have a honeymoon trip coming up in a month...Madrid, Athens and the east coast of Italy, but that will close the travel universe down for a while. I am hanging with about 850,000 frequent flyer miles, so if I need to go, I can. But I want to stay home, just want to chill, teach, practice and serve. And be with Kathy and Koko. Not having to go anywhere. The deck, the yoga platform, the mountains in my back yard. And think about my last 3+ plus years at Sattva. All the people, from the world over, lifetime friends. The learning that changed my life, my incredible friendship with my Guru Deva and my attachment to Ma India. These are memories that can be pondered for the balance of my life.

My goodness, the WhatsApp group exploded with posts and photos as I was ending my trip. Everyone was already missing each other. We had bonded.

I guess I need to apologize to so many in the tribe. I ended up writing 30,000+ words. It took concentrated effort and, sadly, time away from fraternizing and fellowship. I spent much more time in my room writing and much less time hanging. It had to be done! I was determined to get a recap of each day, and it was tough. If I let it go for a day or two, the details would begin to slip away. I needed it all to come in fresh and clear, attempting to not leave anything untouched.

Every time I found time to chat, all of the wonder of the backstories of this group were incredible to hear. Everyone had come from a special place with full lives that led them to this moment at Sattva and the Himalayan Journey. Like Dave told me today, he feels we can all look forward to the documentary, where Adam will work his magic and unfold some tales about many of us.

Of course, this had to all be reported from a personal perspective. I have not developed "the eye in the sky" writing technique. All of you can outline what happened from your own perspectives, easy enough. And certainly, we will have the most full and complete observations from Adam and his crew, who were there 24/7. In ten planned episodes, I don't think they will skip over much. Their photographic diaries will fill in for the loss of adjectives I had describing the beauty that unfolded every day in the mountains, monasteries and hearts of all of us. It is my hope that this retrospective will just fill in some of the cracks in stories that might end up on their editing floor.

Om Mani Padme Hum!

To find out more about The Sattva Yoga Academy, please visit:

www.sattvayogaacademy.com

Or enquire: info@sattvayogaacademy.com

Words from Fellow Wheels of Awakening Pilgrims

Jen Wang...

I've told every friend who's asked that *Wheels of Awakening* was the best trip I've ever taken. No one is surprised by that.
"You say that every trip," they tease, with affection.

But what does surprise them is my follow-up:
"It was so good I'm fine if I never have a better one."

For someone who's made it a point to live each year better than the last, that's new.

Since returning to the place I currently call home, I've realized why. On this journey, I was present enough to notice what a joy *every second of being* can be.

The tingling strain of altitude on my body? Strange, but exhilarating.
The shock of Pangong Lake's icy water at 4,200 meters? Uncomfortable, yet delightful.
Jet lag? Irrelevant, once every morning's gifts began to arrive.
The uncertainty of the schedule? Hilarious, really, because the day was never going to be anything *but* perfect.

So what made this possible? What was here that hadn't been present in all my many beautiful travels before?

Sangha. The utter certainty of a good conversation over chai with whoever happened to be beside me. The frequent shared laughter with helmets both on and off. The wonder of realizing that when people gather with the intention to evolve, transformation doesn't need to be chased. It just…happens.

And **surrender.** This is the season of my life for liberation and letting go. Riding as a passenger gave me the chance to experience that surrender fully (at my preferred pace of 80-100km an hour no less!). Many, many thanks to the seven kings who carried me.

If there's one discovery I treasure most, it's this: Transformation doesn't always arrive as fire and fracture. Sometimes it comes as laughter and companionship. When community, intention, and wisdom align, change becomes effortless. To have one or two is marvelous. To have all three? Catalytic. Like that moment you first "pop" in a journey led by Anand-ji.

What a road. What a life. What a sangha.

Graham…

For me, Tom, as for many of us, it was such a profound experience. The camaraderie of the people and the energy was beyond belief. Very powerful.

It has definitely changed me as a person. I let go of a lot of stuff that was weighing me down. And my relationship with Anand Ji has become a lot closer. I had several silent moments with him where my energy shifted.

I never thought that I would be, in such wonderful company. On an adventure that will certainly be, an epic journey led by Anand Ji.

It's important that I note,
a man that gave me this wonderful quote.

"The universe put a light within me, show me how to let it shine."

Ryan you will always be, a shining light for all eternity.
A man of great peace and understanding, and not in any way demanding.
We never met but wish we could, to let you know that you did good.
You will always be there in my heart, and know you were with us at the start.

So the journey has only just begun, flying to Leh via Dehradun.
We were greeted at Rewa, our home for the night, and paired with our motorcycles shiny and bright.

We traveled to lands far and wide, and were all amazed how our little bikes survived.
The roads were full of challenges for all, but they certainly did enthrall
The stunning scenery and snow topped peaks, monasteries so ancient we could hear them speak.
And all the time the energy and light of the sangha, helped us let go of the fear and anger.

Our greatest challenge yet Khardunla, the highest pass by bike or car.
Euphoria at the challenge met, but wait it wasn't over yet.
Many other beautiful locations,
too many for me all to mention.

You all have your own personal memories to reflect on in parts.

And wisdom talks that really touched our hearts.
Our final high destination a vast water mass, Pangong lake via Nubra Valley and Chang la pass, beauty unsurpassed.

And so the long journey home, to Sattva where we can contemplate and roam .
But wait one final twist awaits, delayed flights, landslides and flood,
but in the end it all came good.

So thank you all for the love you share, and the wonderful Sattva team who are beyond compare.
For Adam and the film crew's efforts, capturing our journey across the deserts.

And finally thank you Anand Ji, for helping me find the inner me.

Much love to you all in your future journeys, I look forward to hearing all of your stories.

Here's to you heroes, you survived and thrived.

Rhonda...

Rhonda Rabbitt awakening to the Guru—
Experiencing the Guru that resides both within and without.
The Guru of love and connection.
The Guru of the space holder, the master, presence.
The Guru of nature—fierce, immense, boundless, soft, flowing, omnipresent and forever changing.
The Guru of friends and of strangers.
The Guru of direct lived experience.

I have known of the Guru.
I have chanted and prayed to the Guru.
I have respected the Guru.
I have looked within for the Guru.
Yet there was a distinction—an awakening, an unquestionable bliss, an inner knowing,
of becoming one with the Guru on this trip.
Forever changed and grateful.
Resonance.

Floris D...

This journey into the Himalyas with Anand Ji and our group was so good at so many levels. And it all just goes on and on.
I always thought children and animals are a lot smarter than adults. But now I have to admit that there are fortunately fellow men and women who really get it and they set a great example. They're living their lives and by that, being an answer.
Thank you Sattva for being there and being a (second) home for so many. From the first to the last day it felt like being home! And doing it this way makes us able to practice and choose to live our lives fearless and free!

Jessica E...

The Wheels of Awakening were set in motion long before arriving at Sattva Yoga Academy for the journey and continue to spin to this day.

My experience was brightened by all the beings of light on the pilgrimage, including you, Tom B. Were it not for other sincere seekers, moments of laughter, awe, wonder and strength wouldn't have been as sticky and sweet—meant to be shared, to be sure. The sacred places and shared events formed as memories and impressions only on account of being surrounded by bright souls sharing in this experience.

Deepest gratitude to our guru, Anand-Ji, for his wisdom and willingness to carry us all through. Sincerest appreciation to Tom B. for cataloguing the experience from your perspective. My husband, Tom E., for your courage and trust, for leaning into and embracing Shakti, and for steering us always toward safety. Boundless bows to the other shore for offering the opportunity for awakening.

Tat Sat

SUGGESTED READING AND MUSIC

Suggested reading:

- The Yoga Sutras by Patanjali
- Autobiography of a Yogi – Paramahansa Yogananda
- Hollywood in the Himalayas – Sadhvi Bhagawati Saraswati*
- Ramayana – various authors and translations
- Bhagavad Gita – various authors and translations
- Liberation – Anand Mehrotra
- This is That – Anand Mehrotra
- Chants of a Lifetime – Krishna Das
- The Journey Home – Swami Radhananda*
- Light on Yoga – B.K.S Iyengar
- Evolution of the Soul – Seane Corn*
- Siddhartha – Herman Hesse
- Narcissus and Goldmund – Herman Hesse
- How to Change Yor Mind – Michael Pollan
- Anything by Baba Ram Das, especially Be Here Now
- The first three books by Carlos Castenada, featuring the teachings of Don Juan
- * Books marked with an asterisk are especially nice on Audio Book

Suggested Music:

I listen to the following four genres over and over:

- Deva Premal and Miten
- Krishna Das
- Shantala
- Chants and music by Tibetan Lamas

Bill and Beth LaShell

Ganga and Gawita

Ben

Sunglass models at the top of the world

Wheels of Awakening men bonding

Wheels of Awakening Women bonding with smoothies

Doing handstands in my record store in Grand Rapids, Michigan

If you would like to reach out to T'Om, he can be reached at tombiehn@live.com A great effort will be made to respond to all inquiries.

WHEELS OF AWARENESS TRIBE

ADAM S	GREGORY C
ALEX K	HENRY Y
ALICE C	KIM T
ANDREW C	ILENIA A
ANNMARIE B	JANICE V
BETH ANNE L	JENNIFER D
CHARLES W	JENNIFER W
CLAIRE Z	JESSICA E
CONNIE C	JOHN A
CORY L	JOSE C
DANIEL M	JOSHUA S
DAPHNE C	JOSHUA B
DAVID S	LEANNE B
ERIC Z	MELISSA B
FLAVIA D	MICHELLE C
FLORIS D	NATHAN B
FRED B	PAUL R
GRAHAM G	PAUL T

PETER L	TATIA C
RAUL G	TAYLOR G
RHONDA R	TERESA C
RODRIGO A	THOMAS C
SAMANTHA J	THOMAS B
SANDRA V	TORSTEN N
SARAH R	MICHEL W
SOPHIE D	BILL L

STAFF AND FILM CREW

ADAM S

ANNEMARIE B

PENNIE N

FAZAL K

JEMINA B

MIGUEL T

REMESH S

RAVI K

SCOTT C

VINEET V

With gratitude to **each and every** one of you whose photos I used in this book. And the gift of YOU that you gave me.

www.ingramcontent.com/pod-product-compliance
Lightning Source LLC
LaVergne TN
LVHW051043080426
835508LV00019B/1671